cooking with

Spice

Contents

A World of Spice

Highly scented seeds, barks, roots, and fruits have been used since ancient times to add aroma and flavor to prepared dishes. In the early centuries of civilization, camels brought these prized spices overland from Asia and India. By medieval times, spices were almost as valuable as gold, and Venice controlled their commerce, becoming a great power in the process. Later, Christopher Columbus was only one of many European explorers who hoped to break the Venetian hold on the spice trade by finding a sea route westward to the spice lands. In his ardor to find new spice routes, the explorer brought these exotic flavorings across oceans, where they contributed to the development of unique ethnic cuisines in the New World. The days of countries waging war over control of the spice routes are long behind us, but spices are still valuable today and impart unique tastes and add complexity to recipes. Only a small amount of spice is needed to add a haunting or heady fragrance and taste to food, both savory and sweet.

The recipes in this book are easy to prepare, whether you are a novice or seasoned home cook. Some are authentic representations of other countries' styles of food, while others are merely inspired by them. Six major cuisines of the world whose culinary traditions embrace the use of spices are represented in these pages: China and Southeast Asia; India; the Middle East and North Africa; Europe; Latin America and the Caribbean; and North America. You can start by cooking your way through the more than fifty recipes inside and then experiment with your new spice collection to create original flavor combinations of your own.

Cinnamon

Allspice

Cardamom

Peppercorns

Nutmeg

Juniper Berries

Cloves

Star Anise

MUST-HAVE SPICES FOR YOUR PANTRY

A wide array of spices is available to home cooks today and the choices can be dizzying. If you are new to cooking with spices, consider this a primer on starting a spice pantry. Having these twenty-five spices on hand in your cupboard means you can create a wealth of dishes influenced by cuisines all over the world.

Whole Spices

Allspice The berry of an evergreen tree, allspice tastes like a combination of cinnamon, nutmeg, and cloves. It is used whole or ground in sweet and savory dishes, including cakes and pies in Europe and North America, in blends for pickling vegetables, and in fiery dishes of the Caribbean region.

Cardamom This intense spice is the dried fruit of a plant in the ginger family. It has an exotic, highly aromatic flavor and is used ground in Indian-style curries, and whole or ground in spiced teas like chai, and in European-style breads and other baked goods. Cardamom is sold in small round pods or as whole or ground black seeds.

Cinnamon In North America, it usually appears in desserts, but cooks in India, Morocco, and Latin and Caribbean countries use cinnamon in sweet and savory dishes alike. The dried bark of a tree, cinnamon grows in Asia, Indonesia, and the West Indies. It has the best flavor in stick form, but you can also purchase it already ground. To grind your own (see page 14), first break or crush the stick into pieces.

Cloves Shaped like a small nail with a round head, the nearly black clove is the dried bud of a tropical evergreen with a strong, sweet flavor and peppery quality. Cloves are used whole or ground in cuisines all over the globe, flavoring curries and tea-based drinks in India, meats and pastries in the Middle East, sausages and sauerkraut in Northern Europe, bean-based soups in Latin America, and classic pickles and baked goods in North America.

Juniper Berries These pea-sized berries from the evergreen juniper bush are blue-black and pungent. They are perhaps best known as the primary flavoring of gin, but they are also used in European countries as marinades for meat and in dishes containing sauerkraut. Use the berries whole, lightly toasted and crushed. Use juniper sparingly; a little goes a long way.

Nutmeg The oval brown seed of a soft fruit, the nutmeg is about ¾ inch (2 cm) long, with a warm, sweet, spicy flavor. A beloved spice in the Western world, nutmeg is used in European style white sauces, such as Béchamel, in spinach-based dishes, and in custard- or fruit-based desserts and cookies in both Europe and North America. Whole nutmeg keeps its flavor much longer than ground nutmeg. Specialized nutmeg graters are available at kitchenware stores, or you can use a rasp-style grater to shave small bits to measure for recipes.

Peppercorns Although small in size, peppercorns pack a wallop of piquancy that is essential to many dishes. Known to help stimulate the appetite, black pepper is ubiquitous around the world. But not all peppercorns are created equal and each will add a subtle difference to your food.

Black & White These are the same spice picked at different stages of ripeness. White peppercorns are slightly milder than their black cousins and are used in light-colored dishes. Always grind pepper fresh before use.

Pink These are not true peppercorns, rather brightly hued berries of a type of rose plant. Slightly sweet, they can be mixed with other peppercorns for a subtle flavor and vibrant color.

Sichuan Though not actually related to true peppercorns, these small dried berries have a bumpy surface, distinct, perfumed fragrance, and citrusy-woodsy flavor. They can be cracked or ground for savory dishes and are typically included in Chinese five-spice powder.

Star Anise A seed-bearing pod from a Chinese evergreen tree related to the magnolia, these brown pods are star-shaped (hence the name) and each pod contains eight seeds. Star anise is used in Asian cuisines to flavor savory dishes and desserts. It is often used whole or snapped into smaller pieces, and it is also ground as one of the spices in Chinese five-spice blend.

Seeds

Coriander This small, light brown seed is actually the dried ripe fruit of fresh coriander, or cilantro. A relative of parsley, its aroma is like a combination of lemon, sage, and caraway. Whole or ground, coriander is a common flavoring for savory dishes in India, Morocco, and the Middle East, where it is often paired with cumin. The best taste comes from whole or freshly ground seeds (page 14).

Cumin The seed of another parsley family member, cumin has a sharp, musky flavor and is used in Indian, Moroccan, and Latin cooking. Cooks in the southern United States also use the spice to make assertive rubs for barbecued meats and to flavor Tex-Mex–style dishes. Cumin is also available ground, but for the best flavor, purchase whole seeds and grind them just before using (page 14).

Dill The dried fruits of the dill plant, dill seeds are flat and light brown in color. The flavor is similar to that of fresh dill leaves, but can be stronger. Dill is used in North America to flavor vegetables and breads. It is often included in packaged pickling spice blends.

Fennel The seed of the common fennel plant, fennel has a licorice-like flavor. European cooks use it for meat dishes, sausage, and fish stews. It is also used in some breads and desserts and, ground, as a component in Chinese five-spice powder. Fennel seeds can be used ground or whole.

Mustard The seeds of the mustard plant come in three colors: yellow (also called white), brown, and black. Yellow is the most common. Mustard seeds have a distinct pungent taste and are used whole in pickled vegetables, whole or ground in Indian-style curried dishes, and ground to flavor spicy dry rubs for meats in the American South.

Sesame This tiny, pointed seed has a nutty flavor that is popular in cuisines all over Asia. It is also a common flavoring for sweet and savory foods in the Middle East and for baked goods in the American South; there, they are sometimes referred to as "benne" seeds. You can find sesame seeds in two forms: white or black; the black seeds have a slightly stronger flavor. Like nuts, oil-rich sesame seeds can turn rancid. Buy them in small quantities and replenish often.

Chile-Based Spices

Cayenne A very hot ground red chile, cayenne is used sparingly in an array of dishes from Indian curries to tandoori-style dishes to spicy Middle Eastern and North African fare. Cooks in the American South also use it to flavor Creole-style dishes, fried chicken, and vegetables. Because different batches vary in heat, and because only a little is needed, always start with a small amount when using cayenne in recipes.

Chile Flakes Also called red pepper flakes, these are the flakes and seeds of small dried red chiles. They're used in cuisines around the world to add bright heat to dishes from stir-fries and curries to soups and pastas to seafood dishes and pickles. Just a pinch or two adds bright heat to any recipe.

Chile Powder Chile powder is a pure powder made by grinding a single variety of dried chile. Ancho and New Mexico chile powders are the most commonly available. Do not confuse these pure powders with "chili powder," typically a blend of powdered dried chiles and other seasonings. If you can't find pure chile powder where you buy your regular spices, look for it in Latin groceries.

Ancho Boasting a deep, slightly sweet, and raisin-like flavor, ancho powder is made from poblano chiles that have been dried and ground. Ancho chile powder has varying heat, from mild to assertive. The color is typically a dark, brick red, though its hue can vary.

New Mexico Made from dried red Anaheim chiles (and sometimes labeled Anaheim chile powder), this offers an earthy yet bright chile flavor. Mild in flavor, it is a good choice for cooks who don't care for a lot of heat, but still enjoy the flavor of dried chiles. Its color ranges from orange to deep red.

Paprika Made from ground dried red peppers, paprika comes in three main types: sweet, half-sweet, and hot. Most of the paprika on the market comes from Hungary and Spain.

Sweet or Hot Sweet paprika is most often used in recipes, so it's a great one to keep on hand to flavor Indian and North African dishes, Hungarian-style chicken dishes or goulashes, or Cajun- or Creole-style dishes. Its color ranges from orange-red to red.

Smoked A Spanish specialty, smoked paprika is made from red chiles that have been smoked and then ground. It has an earthy, smoky, almost meaty flavor and deep red color.

Sesame Seeds

Dill Seeds

Smoked Paprika

Sweet Paprika

New Mexico Chile Powder

Ancho Chile Powder

Cumin Seeds

Fennel Seeds

Chile Flakes

Mustard Seeds

Coriander Seeds

Cayenne

Ground Ginger

Madras Curry Powder

Garlic Powder

Atlantic Seafood Seasoning

Garam Masala

Ground Turmeric

Chinese Five-Spice

Aromatic Spices

Garlic Powder Garlic powder is made by dehydrating and then finely grinding garlic flakes. While fresh garlic is often the best choice for many recipes, garlic powder is a good item to keep on hand if you enjoy highly spiced Middle Eastern food or bold, spice-crusted Cajun, Creole, or barbecue fare.

Ground Ginger Indispensable in Asian cooking, the warm, perfumed taste and spicy heat of ground ginger is also a favorite flavoring of North American and British cooks, usually featured in desserts. Ground ginger is a common addition to Indian-style curry blends and Moroccan-style seasoning mixtures and is a welcome addition to fruit or pumpkin pies and holiday cookies.

Ground Turmeric The root of a plant belonging to the ginger family, turmeric is valued both for its taste and its bright yellow color. It is commonly used to flavor Southeast Asian, Indian, and Moroccan and North African cuisines and is one of the main ingredients in Indian-style curry powder.

Spice Blends

Chinese Five-Spice This classic Chinese spice mixture is an aromatic blend of five different spices. The proportions and quantities differ, depending on the source, but typical mixtures include ground fennel, cloves, cinnamon, Sichuan peppercorns, and star anise. Five-spice powder is used for marinades, glazes, and long-cooked stews, and it also comes to the table mixed with coarse salt as a dipping condiment for roasted meats.

Curry Powder In South Asia, dried spices are roasted, ground, and then blended into complex mixes, known as masalas, to flavor sauces. The spice mixes vary by region and dish, from mild and aromatic to assertively spicy. Many cooks in Asia prefer to prepare their own unique curry spice blend. But in Britain and North America, it is common to see prepackaged blends, usually boasting a bright yellow color from the high proportion of turmeric in the mix. Curry powder labeled "Madras" refers to a commonly available, all-purpose mixture. It can be used as a standard curry blend for Indian-inspired dishes from Japan, China, and Southeast Asia.

If you enjoy the flavor of curry spice blends, there are many more types available with which you can experiment. For example, African curry has mild heat with hints of citrus; Japanese curry is complex with a slight sweetness; vadouvan curry, popular in French cooking, is mild with a delicate complexity and a hint of tangy spice; and vindaloo curry has a sweet-and-tangy flavor, bright, peppery finish, and moderate heat perfect for preparing the spicy namesake stew.

Garam Masala This dried spice mixture, made popular in northern India, typically includes cinnamon, fenugreek, cumin, peppercorns, and cardamom, although, like curry powder, each home cook or restaurant chef typically creates his or her own custom blend. Garam masala is used in curry-style dishes throughout India and Southeast Asia. It is also sometimes sprinkled on dishes as a finishing spice just before serving.

Atlantic Seafood Seasoning This zesty, complex spice blend finds it way into many dishes, especially shellfish recipes. Perhaps the most famous of this type of seasoning blend is Old Bay, a staple of the mid-Atlantic cooking of North America. The exact proportions of Old Bay and other seafood seasonings vary, but the mixture typically includes ground mustard seeds, red chile flakes, black pepper, cloves, allspice, ginger, cardamom, cinnamon, and paprika, along with other proprietary spices and dried herbs.

TOASTING SPICES

To intensify their flavor, toast spices in a dry skillet. It is best to toast whole spices and seeds before grinding, but ground spices can also be toasted if you keep a close eye on them, as they burn easily.

step one
Put the spices in a small, heavy, dry skillet.

step two
Toast over medium heat, stirring constantly, until fragrant; some spices will turn a shade or two darker.

step three
Immediately pour the spices from the pan onto a plate to stop the cooking.

step four
Let cool before using, about 10 minutes.

SPICE BASICS

Spices are simple to work with, but require a little care to be sure they retain their maximum flavor and aromatic qualities. To ensure freshness, seek out spices from a quality source that has high turnover.

Buying Ideally, spices should be purchased whole and then ground just before use. Some spices are only available ground. In either case, buy your spices in the smallest amounts you can, as they lose flavor over time.

Storing Keep spices in tightly closed containers in a cool, dark place that is ideally not beside the stove or elsewhere in a bright kitchen. If you buy spices in bulk, purchase glass spice jars for storing. Whole spices will last for about 1 year, ground spices for about 6 months.

Grinding For grinding small quantities of spices, use a mortar and pestle or a pepper mill reserved for spices. Or buy a small electric coffee grinder and use it only for grinding spices. Grind only the amount you need. Turn to page 13 for instructions on toasting spices.

Cooking Many recipes call for heating ground spices in oil prior to incorporating them into a recipe. Opinions vary on the usefulness of this technique, but many cooks feel that the oil helps "bloom" the spice and brings out its flavor. Combining a ground spice with oil also helps it to more readily dissolve into other mixtures.

SPICE UP YOUR DINNER

You can add global flavor to many types of food by sprinkling lightly with ground spices, salt, pepper, and other flavorings, tossing with olive oil, and then sautéing, roasting, or grilling. Try the ideas below, or make up your own custom combinations.

Indian-Style Chicken

cumin
coriander
turmeric

Asian-Style Leafy Greens

sesame seeds
chile flakes
soy sauce

Moroccan-Style Vegetables

cinnamon
ginger
turmeric
lemon juice

Caribbean-Style Pork

allspice
cinnamon
cayenne
lime juice

Latin-Style Seafood

chile powder
cumin
lime juice

BBQ-Style Shrimp

mustard
garlic powder
paprika
lemon juice

China &
Southeast Asia

Beef Satay with
Coconut-Peanut Sauce 19

Wok-Seared Salt & Pepper Shrimp 20

Chinese-Style Braised Short Ribs 22

Braised Pork & Eggplant 23

Chicken with Tangerines
& Star Anise 25

Garden Peas with Sesame
& Garlic 26

Baby Bok Choy with Chile
& Sesame 27

Spiced Poached Pears 28

- 1¾ lb (875 g) beef chuck, trimmed and cubed
- 1½ tsp curry powder
- 3 Tbsp canola oil
- Salt and freshly ground black peppercorns
- 2 Tbsp minced yellow onion
- 4 cloves garlic, minced
- ½ tsp hot red pepper sauce
- 1 Tbsp brown sugar
- 1 Tbsp fresh lime juice
- ½ cup (2½ oz/75 g) toasted peanuts, finely chopped
- 1 cup (8 fl oz/250 ml) unsweetened coconut milk
- 1 Tbsp minced fresh cilantro
- Lime wedges for finishing

6
SERVINGS

Beef Satay with Coconut-Peanut Sauce

curry powder
peppercorns

Soak 12 bamboo skewers in water to cover. In a large bowl, combine beef cubes with curry powder, 1 tablespoon of oil, ½ teaspoon salt, and plenty of pepper. Toss to coat beef evenly. Let stand while you make sauce.

To make peanut sauce, in a frying pan, heat remaining 2 tablespoons oil over medium heat. Add onion and cook, stirring, until softened but not browned, about 5 minutes. Add garlic and cook for 1 minute more. Stir in red pepper sauce, brown sugar, lime juice, and peanuts. Season with ¼ teaspoon salt and a pinch of pepper. Stir in coconut milk and continue to cook, stirring frequently, until thickened, 6–8 minutes. Remove from heat and stir in cilantro.

Prepare a grill for direct grilling over medium-high heat, or preheat a stove-top grill pan over medium-high heat. If using a grill, brush and oil grill rack. Drain skewers. Thread beef cubes onto skewers, dividing them evenly and pressing them together snugly. Wrap 2 inches (5 cm) of blunt end of each skewer with aluminum foil to make a handle. Place skewers on grill rack directly over hot coals or heat elements, or place in grill pan, and cook, turning with tongs, until meat is firm but still has a little give, 3½–4 minutes per side. Transfer to a platter and let rest, loosely covered, for 3–4 minutes.

Remove foil from skewers. Squeeze a little lime juice over top and serve right away with sauce on side.

For this modern interpretation of an Indonesian dish, choose high-quality curry powder, such as Madras. The spice-dusted meat is simply grilled so that the curry flavor will shine through. The coconut milk–based dipping sauce uses chopped peanuts instead of peanut butter for a textural contrast to the chewy steak.

6–8 SERVINGS

Wok-Seared Salt & Pepper Shrimp

black, pink & Sichuan peppercorns

1 tsp mixed black, pink, and Sichuan peppercorns

2 lb (1 kg) medium shrimp in the shell

Sea salt

2 Tbsp canola oil

4 cloves garlic, minced

Lemon wedges for serving

Using a mortar and pestle, finely crush peppercorns.

In a bowl, combine shrimp, half of peppercorns, and 1 teaspoon salt and toss together. Set aside.

In a wok or large frying pan, heat oil over high heat. Add garlic, remaining peppercorns, and 1 teaspoon salt and cook, stirring, for 1 minute. Add shrimp and cook, stirring, until opaque throughout, 3–4 minutes. Serve right away with lemon wedges, with a small bowl for discarded shells alongside.

This casual appetizer calls for just six ingredients and a few minutes of your time, so it's important that your spices and other ingredients are at the peak of freshness. The mixture of black, pink, and Sichuan peppercorns creates a sweet-citrusy-peppery flavor that perfectly complements briny shellfish.

4–6
SERVINGS

Chinese-Style Braised Short Ribs

*Chinese five-spice powder
star anise*

3½ lb (1.75 kg) beef short ribs

½ cup (4 fl oz/125 ml) hoisin sauce

¼ cup (2 fl oz/60 ml) soy sauce

¼ cup (2 fl oz/60 ml) dry sherry

3 Tbsp honey

3 Tbsp Asian sesame oil

2 Tbsp peeled and grated fresh ginger

1 Tbsp Chinese five-spice powder

1 Tbsp Dijon mustard

4 star anise pods

2 cloves garlic, minced

1 red jalapeño chile, seeded and minced

1 bunch green onions, thinly sliced

Fresh cilantro leaves

This Chinese-influenced recipe mingles star anise and five-spice powder with other Eastern and Western ingredients to create sweet-and-spicy comfort food perfect for a cold night. Although the cooking is mostly hands-off, you'll need to plan ahead, as the meat marinates for several hours and needs a couple of hours in the oven.

Arrange ribs in a single layer in a nonreactive dish. In a bowl, whisk together hoisin sauce, soy sauce, sherry, honey, sesame oil, ginger, five-spice powder, mustard, star anise, garlic, and chile. Pour over ribs and turn to coat well. Cover and marinate in refrigerator for at least 4 hours or up to overnight.

Remove ribs from refrigerator and bring to room temperature. Preheat oven to 350°F (180°C).

Place ribs in a 5½- to 7-qt (5.5- to 7-l) Dutch oven or braiser and pour marinade over the top. Cover pot and bake for 1 hour. Uncover and continue to bake for 30 minutes. Turn over ribs and cook until meat is very tender, sauce has thickened, and ribs are coated with a sticky brown glaze, about 30 minutes longer.

Remove from oven, cover, and let stand for 5 minutes. Sprinkle ribs with green onions and cilantro and serve right away.

Braised Pork & Eggplant

**Chinese five-spice powder
peppercorns**

4 Tbsp (2 fl oz/60 ml)
canola oil

1½ lb (750 g) boneless pork
shoulder, trimmed and cubed

⅓ cup (3 fl oz/80 ml)
soy sauce

¼ cup (2 fl oz/60 ml)
dry sherry

2 Tbsp brown sugar

1 tsp Chinese
five-spice powder

Freshly ground black
peppercorns

½ tsp cornstarch

½ lb (250 g) Asian
eggplants, cubed

4 thin slices peeled
fresh ginger

2 green onions,
thinly sliced

4 cloves garlic, minced

Steamed rice for serving

Heat a Dutch oven or large, deep frying pan over high heat until
very hot. Add 2 tablespoons of oil. Add pork in single layer and
sear until golden on all sides, 8–10 minutes total. Using slotted
spoon, transfer pork to a plate.

In a large bowl, stir together 2 cups (16 fl oz/500 ml) water, soy
sauce, sherry, brown sugar, five-spice powder, a few grinds of
pepper and cornstarch. Set aside.

Return pan to high heat and add remaining 2 tablespoons oil.
Add eggplant and sauté until lightly browned and beginning
to soften, about 5 minutes. Transfer to a bowl. Return pan to
medium heat, add ginger, green onions, and garlic and sauté
until aromatic, about 10 seconds. Pour in soy sauce mixture,
bring to boil, and stir in seared pork cubes. Cover pot, reduce
heat to low, and cook until pork is tender, about 1 hour.

Uncover, add reserved eggplant, and simmer until eggplant
is tender and flavors are blended, 10–15 minutes. Transfer to
serving bowl and serve right away with rice.

This recipe is a good example of
how just a small amount of
Chinese five-spice powder can
permeate an entire dish. Soy
sauce, sherry, and a touch of
brown sugar help balance the
flavors. With chunks of pork and
cubes of eggplant, it's a perfect
savory one-dish meal when
served over rice.

2 tangerines

8 skin-on, bone-in, chicken thighs (about 3¼ lb/1.6 kg)

Salt and freshly ground black peppercorns

2 Tbsp canola oil

1 small yellow onion, finely chopped

2 cloves garlic, minced

¼-inch (6-mm) piece fresh ginger, peeled and grated

1 cup (8 fl oz/250 ml) low-sodium chicken broth

2 Tbsp soy sauce

1 tsp Sriracha sauce

2 star anise pods

2 tsp cornstarch

Steamed rice for serving

Chicken with Tangerines & Star Anise

**peppercorns
star anise**

Finely grate zest from tangerines, then squeeze ½ cup tangerine juice. Season chicken with 1 teaspoon salt and ½ teaspoon pepper.

In Dutch oven or other heavy pot with lid, heat oil over medium-high heat until very hot but not smoking. Working in batches, add chicken and cook, turning once or twice, until browned on both sides, about 9 minutes per batch. Transfer to plate.

Pour off all but 1 tablespoon fat from pot and return pot to medium heat. Add onion and cook, stirring occasionally, until softened, 3–4 minutes. Add garlic, ginger, and half of tangerine zest and stir until fragrant, about 1 minute. Add broth, tangerine juice, soy sauce, Sriracha sauce, and star anise and bring to a boil, scraping up browned bits from pot bottom. Return chicken thighs to pot, reduce heat to low, cover, and simmer until chicken shows no sign of pink when pierced with tip of a sharp knife near bone, about 25 minutes.

Transfer chicken to a warmed platter. Remove and discard star anise. Bring liquid in pot to boil over medium-high heat. In small bowl, mix cornstarch and 1 tablespoon water. Stir cornstarch mixture into liquid in pot and cook just until sauce thickens slightly, about 30 seconds.

Pour sauce over the chicken. Sprinkle with remaining tangerine zest and serve right away with rice.

Here, fresh tangerines (at their best in winter) add a tart-sweet element to a star anise-infused braising liquid for chicken. The fragrant ingredients perk up the deep flavors in the dish and cut through the richness of tender braised chicken thighs. If you like, sauté tangerine wedges in butter for a pretty garnish.

Garden Peas with Sesame & Garlic

peppercorns
sesame seeds

2 Tbsp sesame seeds
3 lb (1.5 kg) English peas, shelled
1 Tbsp olive oil

1 tsp Asian sesame oil
2 cloves garlic, minced
Salt and freshly ground black peppercorns

In a dry pan, toast sesame seeds over medium heat, watching carefully, until golden brown and fragrant, 4–5 minutes. Pour onto a plate and set aside to cool.

Bring large pot of salted water to a boil. Fill large bowl two-thirds full with ice water. Add peas to boiling water and cook briefly, 2–3 minutes. Drain peas and immediately plunge into ice water. Let stand for 1 minute, then drain.

In large frying pan over medium-high heat, warm olive and sesame oils. When oils are hot, add garlic and sauté, stirring constantly, until fragrant but not brown, about 30 seconds.

Add peas and a pinch each of salt and pepper and sauté, tossing and stirring occasionally, until peas are just tender, 3–4 minutes. Sprinkle with toasted sesame seeds and stir well. Taste and adjust seasonings. Serve right away.

This is a great example of how spices can add an exotic flair to everyday market ingredients. In this case, toasted sesame seeds, reinforced by fragrant sesame oil, lend Asian flavors to simply sautéed spring peas, a dish that's usually seen in England and North America.

1 Tbsp sesame seeds

4 heads baby bok choy (about 1 lb/500 g total weight)

1½ Tbsp canola oil

3 cloves garlic, thinly sliced

½ tsp chile flakes

Salt

¼ cup (2 fl oz/60 ml) chicken broth

2 tsp Asian chile oil

Baby Bok Choy with Chile & Sesame

chile flakes
sesame seeds

In a dry pan, toast sesame seeds over medium heat, watching carefully, until golden brown and fragrant, 4–5 minutes. Pour onto a plate and set aside to cool.

Cut off tough base from each head of bok choy. Separate heads into individual stalks by snapping stalks away from their cores.

In a wok or large frying pan, heat oil over medium-high heat. Add garlic and chile flakes and cook, tossing and stirring constantly, until fragrant but not browned, 20–30 seconds. Add bok choy and a pinch of salt and cook, tossing and stirring, until bok choy just begins to wilt, 1–2 minutes.

Add broth and cook, stirring occasionally, until bok choy is just tender and broth evaporates, 1–2 minutes. Add chile oil, stir well to coat bok choy, and remove from heat.

Stir in toasted sesame seeds, transfer mixture to a warmed serving bowl, and serve right away.

Here is another example of how a small amount of spices, in this case, nutty sesame seeds and fiery chile flakes, can enliven mild vegetables. You can also try this technique with other leafy greens such as Swiss chard, kale, or broccoli rabe.

Spiced Poached Pears

6 SERVINGS

cinnamon
star anise

1 cup (8 oz/250 g) sugar
1 cinnamon stick
3 star anise pods

4 thin slices fresh ginger
6 Bosc pears, peeled

In a saucepan that will hold the pears snugly, bring 4 cups (32 fl oz/1 l) water to a boil over medium heat. Add sugar, cinnamon, star anise, and ginger and simmer, stirring, until sugar has dissolved, about 4 minutes.

Add peeled pears to pan. When liquid has almost returned to a boil, reduce heat to medium-low and simmer gently, uncovered, until pears are tender when pierced with a knife, 15–20 minutes. Remove from heat and let pears cool in syrup.

Divide pears among individual serving bowls. Spoon some of cooled syrup over each pear. Serve at room temperature.

Cinnamon stick and star anise are infused into a simple syrup to form a fragrant poaching medium for fresh fall pears. The fruit simmers gently in the spiced syrup and becomes tender while the spiced liquid infuses into the fruit. Try this as a refreshing dessert after a rich meal.

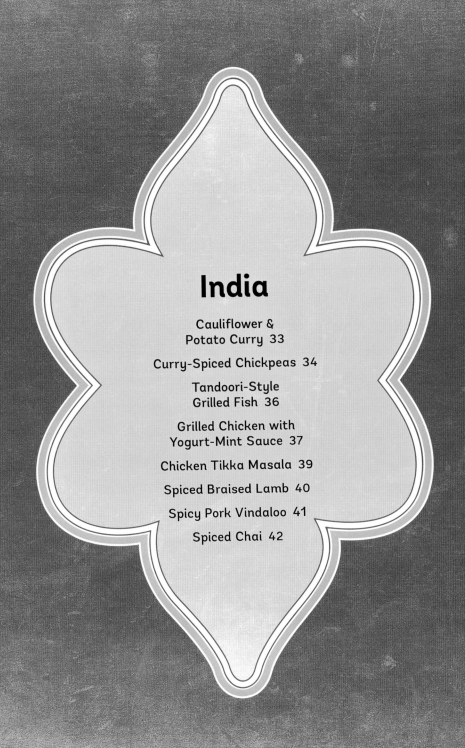

India

Cauliflower &
Potato Curry 33

Curry-Spiced Chickpeas 34

Tandoori-Style
Grilled Fish 36

Grilled Chicken with
Yogurt-Mint Sauce 37

Chicken Tikka Masala 39

Spiced Braised Lamb 40

Spicy Pork Vindaloo 41

Spiced Chai 42

½ cup (4 fl oz/125 ml) canola oil

1 lb (500 g) small red-skinned potatoes, halved

1 head cauliflower, cut into florets

1 large yellow onion, coarsely chopped

1-inch (2.5-cm) piece fresh ginger, peeled and grated

1-inch (2.5-cm) piece cinnamon stick

2 tsp ground cumin

2 tsp ground coriander

2 tsp brown mustard seeds

1 tsp ground cardamom

1 tsp ground turmeric

½ tsp cayenne pepper

1 cup (8 oz/250 g) plain yogurt (not Greek style)

Salt

6 oz (185 g) frozen baby peas

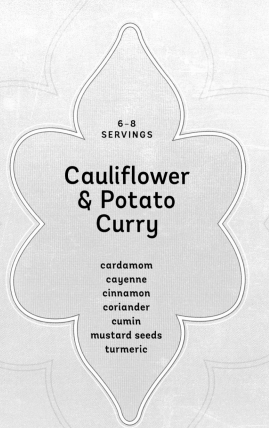

6–8
SERVINGS

Cauliflower & Potato Curry

**cardamom
cayenne
cinnamon
coriander
cumin
mustard seeds
turmeric**

In a Dutch oven, heat canola oil over medium-high heat until shimmering. Working in batches to avoid overcrowding, add potatoes and cauliflower and sauté until potatoes are golden brown and cauliflower florets are speckled with golden brown, 5–7 minutes per batch. Remove from pan and set aside.

Add onion to pan and sauté over medium-high heat until caramel brown, 12–15 minutes. Stir in ginger, cinnamon, cumin, coriander, mustard seeds, cardamom, turmeric, and cayenne, and sauté until spices are fragrant and coat chopped onion, about 1 minute. Add 1 cup (8 fl oz/250 ml) hot water and deglaze pan, stirring and scraping up browned bits on bottom of pan with a wooden spoon. Stir in yogurt and 2 teaspoons salt, reduce heat to medium, and cook until onion-yogurt mixture starts to simmer, about 5 minutes.

Partially cover and cook over low heat until vegetables are tender and sauce is thick, about 20 minutes. Gently stir in peas and cook for about 10 minutes longer.

Remove cinnamon stick and serve right away.

This savory vegetable dish is influenced by the cuisine of northern India, where curries are typically mild in flavor and served in a creamy, yogurt-based sauce. This is a good example of how cooks customize their own curry blend instead of using premixed powders. Feel free to alter the proportions to your own taste.

India
33

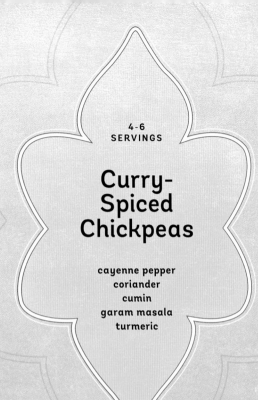

Curry-Spiced Chickpeas

cayenne pepper
coriander
cumin
garam masala
turmeric

2 cans (15 oz/470 g each) chickpeas

1 small yellow onion, chopped

2 Tbsp peeled and chopped fresh ginger

3 cloves garlic, chopped

1 jalapeño chile, seeded and minced

2 Tbsp canola oil

1 Tbsp ground cumin

1 tsp ground coriander

1 tsp ground turmeric

1 tsp garam masala

⅛ tsp cayenne pepper

½ cup (3 oz/90 g) chopped tomatoes

1 Tbsp fresh lemon juice

Salt

1 Tbsp chopped fresh cilantro

This dish is based on a northern Indian snack. Serve it as part of a vegetarian feast or as a side dish for roasted meats or poultry. Chickpeas' neutral flavor is a good carrier for spices, which are layered here for a bold flavor, then refreshed with lemon juice and chopped cilantro leaves.

Drain chickpeas into a colander, rinse under cold running water, and drain again. Set aside.

In a mini food processor or mortar, combine onion, ginger, garlic, and chile and process or grind with a pestle to a smooth paste. Add 2–3 tablespoons water if needed to facilitate grinding.

In a large saucepan, heat oil over medium-high heat. Add onion paste and sauté just until it begins to brown, 5–7 minutes. Stir in cumin, coriander, turmeric, garam masala, and cayenne and sauté for a few seconds. Add tomatoes and 1 cup (8 fl oz/250 ml) water and bring to a boil. Add chickpeas, reduce heat to low, and stir in lemon juice and 1 teaspoon salt. Cover and cook, stirring occasionally, until sauce has thickened, about 15 minutes.

Transfer chickpeas to a bowl, garnish with cilantro, and serve right away.

4 SERVINGS

Tandoori-Style Grilled Fish

cayenne
garam masala
peppercorns

Tandoori-style cooking calls for marinating foods in yogurt and spices and then cooking them over intense heat. This version pairs cinnamon- and cardamom-scented garam masala with fiery cayenne pepper in a marinade for mild fish and then offers an easy cucumber salad as a cooling accompaniment.

⅓ cup (3 oz/90 g) plain yogurt

4 Tbsp (2 fl oz/60 ml) fresh lemon juice

1 Tbsp garam masala

2 cloves garlic, minced

1 Tbsp peeled and grated fresh ginger

Salt and freshly ground black peppercorns

¼ tsp cayenne pepper

4 skin-on Arctic char fillets, 6 oz (185 g) each

1 cucumber, peeled and thinly sliced

½ red onion, thinly sliced

2 cups (14 oz/440 g) seeded and finely chopped tomato

3 Tbsp olive oil

2 Tbsp minced fresh cilantro

In a large nonreactive bowl, stir together yogurt, 2 tablespoons of lemon juice, garam masala, garlic, ginger, ½ teaspoon salt, a pinch of black pepper, and cayenne. Add fish fillets, coating them with marinade. Cover and refrigerate for 2 hours.

While fish marinates, in a bowl, toss together cucumber, onion, tomato, remaining 2 tablespoons lemon juice, ½ teaspoon salt, a pinch of black pepper, 1 tablespoon of oil, and 1 tablespoon of cilantro. Cover and refrigerate until serving time.

Position oven rack in uppermost position and preheat broiler. Line bottom of a broiler pan with aluminum foil and place rack on top. Remove fish from marinade and brush away excess marinade. Drizzle fillets with remaining 2 tablespoons oil and season lightly with salt and pepper. Arrange fillets on prepared pan so they aren't touching. Broil until fish is opaque throughout, about 4 minutes. Remove fish from oven, cover with foil, and let rest for 2 minutes.

Serve right away with cucumber salad alongside. Garnish with remaining 1 tablespoon cilantro.

2 lemons

4 whole chicken legs, about 12 oz (375 g) each

Salt and freshly ground black peppercorns

2 cloves garlic

1 small yellow onion, coarsely chopped

2 cups (16 oz/500 g) plain yogurt

1 Tbsp curry powder

1 tsp sweet paprika

1/4 tsp ground cinnamon

1/8 tsp cayenne pepper

Canola oil for grilling

1 cucumber, peeled, seeded, and coarsely grated

1 Tbsp chopped fresh mint, plus leaves for garnish

Grilled Chicken with Yogurt-Mint Sauce

cayenne
cinnamon
curry powder
peppercorns
sweet paprika

Squeeze 2 tablespoons juice from 1 lemon. Cut remaining lemon into 8 wedges and set aside. Place chicken in a large nonreactive baking dish and sprinkle evenly with lemon juice and 3/4 teaspoon salt. Cover and refrigerate for 1 hour.

With a food processor running, drop garlic cloves through feed tube to chop them. Stop motor, add onion, and pulse until puréed. Add 1 cup (8 oz/250 g) of yogurt, curry powder, paprika, cinnamon, and cayenne and pulse to combine. Pour mixture over chicken and mix well. Cover and refrigerate for at least 4 hours or up to 12 hours.

Prepare a grill for indirect grilling (1 hot zone and 1 cool zone) over medium-high heat. Brush and oil grill rack.

Remove each chicken leg from yogurt mixture and shake gently to remove excess marinade. Place chicken, skin side down, on cool side of grill. Cover grill and cook until an instant-read thermometer inserted in thickest part of thigh away from bone registers 170°F (77°C), 30–35 minutes. Meanwhile, in a small bowl, mix remaining 1 cup yogurt, cucumber, and chopped mint until blended. Season to taste with salt and black pepper. Cover and refrigerate until serving.

When chicken is ready, transfer to a warmed platter and let rest for 5 minutes. Sprinkle with mint leaves. Serve right away. Pass yogurt sauce and lemon wedges at table.

Here is another tandoori-style dish that features curry powder in a yogurt-based marinade, which at once flavors the chicken legs and ensures they stay moist during high-heat grilling. Cinnamon, sweet paprika, and cayenne pepper bolster the curry flavors while a yogurt-based dipping sauce helps temper the heat.

- ¼ cup (2 oz/60 g) plain yogurt (not Greek style)
- Juice from 1½ limes
- 3 tsp peeled and grated fresh ginger
- 2 tsp ground cumin
- 1¼ tsp garam masala
- 2 tsp sweet or hot paprika
- 4 skinless, boneless chicken breast halves
- Salt
- 5 Tbsp (3 fl oz/80 ml) canola oil
- 5 cardamom pods
- 1 small yellow onion, finely chopped
- 1 clove garlic, minced
- 1 tsp ground coriander
- ½ tsp ground turmeric
- 1 lb (500 g) tomatoes, peeled, seeded, and chopped
- 1 jalapeño chile, thinly sliced
- ½ cup (4 fl oz/125 ml) heavy cream
- Juice from ½ lemon
- Steamed rice for serving

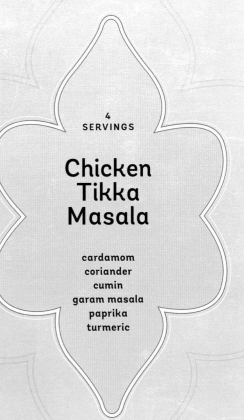

4 SERVINGS

Chicken Tikka Masala

cardamom
coriander
cumin
garam masala
paprika
turmeric

In a glass bowl, stir together yogurt, lime juice, 2 teaspoons of ginger, 1 teaspoon of cumin, 1 teaspoon of garam masala, and paprika. Trim excess fat from chicken and cut into 1-inch (2.5-cm) cubes. Add to yogurt mixture, stir, cover, and refrigerate for at least 1 hour or up to 7 hours.

Preheat a stove top grill pan over medium-high heat. Remove chicken from marinade, shake off excess, and place on a plate. Season to taste with salt and drizzle with 2 tablespoons oil; toss to coat. Cook, turning once, until browned, about 6 minutes.

Gently crack cardamom pods with side of a chef's knife. Remove seeds and grind to a coarse powder (see page 14); discard pods. In a saucepan, heat remaining 3 tablespoons oil over medium heat. Add onion, remaining 1 teaspoon ginger, and garlic and sauté until onion is soft, 4–5 minutes. Add ground cardamom, remaining 1 teaspoon cumin, coriander, and turmeric and sauté for 2 minutes. Add tomatoes and sauté until oil separates from tomato mixture, 5–8 minutes. Add chile, cream, and ½ cup (4 fl oz/125 ml) water, bring to a boil, reduce heat to low, and simmer until a creamy sauce forms, 8–10 minutes. Stir in cooked chicken and remaining ¼ teaspoon garam masala, season to taste with salt, and simmer until chicken is cooked through, 8–10 minutes. Stir in lemon juice. Serve right away with rice.

Tikka masala is wildly popular in Britain, where Indian food has become a major part of the national cuisine. Every recipe is different, but common elements include heavy cream, tomatoes, and a lively blend of curry-style spices. Serve the spicy stew with warm naan or pita bread for dipping, if desired.

4 SERVINGS

Spiced Braised Lamb

cinnamon
coriander
curry powder

This satisfying lamb dish supplements curry powder with additional coriander and cinnamon, lending a sweet-scented accent that works well with the strongly flavored meat. For a heartier dish, stir in ½ pound (250 g) cubed red-skinned potatoes during the last 20 minutes of cooking.

1 yellow onion, chopped
2 Tbsp peeled and chopped fresh ginger
3 cloves garlic, chopped
1 small jalapeño chile, seeded and minced
1 Tbsp ground coriander
1 tsp curry powder
¼ tsp ground cinnamon
2 lb (1 kg) boneless lamb shoulder, cubed
Salt
3 Tbsp canola oil
1 cup (8 oz/250 g) plain yogurt
Steamed rice for serving

In a blender, combine onion, ginger, garlic, and chile and process to a paste. In a small bowl, stir together coriander, curry powder, and cinnamon.

Season lamb with 1 teaspoon salt. Heat a Dutch oven over high heat until very hot and add 2 tablespoons of oil. Add lamb in a single layer, working in batches if necessary to avoid crowding, and sear, turning once, until browned on all sides, 8–10 minutes per batch. Using a slotted spoon, transfer lamb to a plate.

Return pan to medium heat and add remaining 1 tablespoon oil. Add onion-garlic paste and sauté just until it begins to brown, about 3 minutes. Stir in spice mixture and sauté 10 seconds longer. Add 2 cups (16 fl oz/500 ml) water and 1 teaspoon salt. Bring to a boil over medium-high heat and then reduce heat to low. Gradually whisk in yogurt until combined with sauce. Return lamb to the pan, cover, and simmer gently until lamb is tender, 60–70 minutes. Taste and adjust seasoning with salt. Serve right away with rice.

Spicy Pork Vindaloo

cayenne
cinnamon
cumin
hot paprika
mustard seeds
peppercorns
turmeric

2½–3 lb (1.25–1.5 kg) boneless pork shoulder, trimmed and cubed

Salt and freshly ground black peppercorns

½ cup (4 fl oz/125 ml) canola oil

2 yellow onions, finely chopped

8 cloves garlic, minced

2-inch (5-cm) piece fresh ginger, peeled and grated

1½ tsp cayenne pepper

1½ tsp brown mustard seeds

1½ tsp ground cumin

1½ tsp hot paprika

1½ tsp ground turmeric

1½ tsp ground cinnamon

Pinch of ground cloves

⅓ cup (3 fl oz/80 ml) white wine vinegar

1 cup (8 fl oz/250 ml) chicken broth

Place pork in a bowl, sprinkle with 1 teaspoon salt and 1 teaspoon black pepper, and toss to coat. In a large frying pan, heat canola oil over medium-high heat. Working in batches, add pork and cook until well browned on all sides, 6–7 minutes per batch. Remove from pan and set aside.

Add onions to pan, raise heat to high, and sauté until browned, 10–12 minutes. Add garlic, ginger, cayenne, mustard seeds, cumin, paprika, turmeric, cinnamon, and cloves and sauté until spices are fragrant and evenly coat chopped onions, about 1 minute. Pour in vinegar and deglaze pan, stirring and scraping up browned bits on bottom of pan with a wooden spoon. Stir in broth and bring to a boil.

Transfer pork to a large Dutch oven and pour in broth mixture. Partially cover and cook over low heat until pork is very tender and sauce has thickened, 1½–2 hours.

Divide pork among warmed plates and serve right away.

Legend has it that vindaloos, the spicy, sweet-sour curries of western coastal India, were influenced by the cuisine of Portugal, of which India was a former colony. Vindaloos have a reputation for being extremely spicy, though this version is on the tame side. If you like a more fiery stew, add additional cayenne pepper.

India
41

Spiced Chai

cardamom
cinnamon
cloves
peppercorns

5 cardamom pods

1 cinnamon stick, plus sticks for garnish (optional)

4 black peppercorns

4 whole cloves

3 cups (24 fl oz/750 ml) whole milk

⅓ cup (⅓ oz/10 g) strong black tea leaves such as Darjeeling or Ceylon

½ cup (4 oz/125 g) sugar

Gently crack cardamom pods with side of a chef's knife. Remove seeds and discard pods. In a mortar, spice grinder, or coffee mill reserved for spices, combine cardamom, cinnamon stick, peppercorns, and cloves and crush with a pestle or grind to a coarse powder.

Transfer spice powder to a large saucepan and add milk and 1 cup (8 fl oz/250 ml) water. Bring to a boil over medium heat, then reduce heat to low and simmer, uncovered, for 10 minutes. Stir tea leaves and sugar into milk mixture, cover, and steep chai over low heat for 5 minutes, or until it reaches desired strength. Remove from heat.

Strain chai through a fine-mesh sieve into warmed cups. Serve right away, garnishing cups with cinnamon sticks, if you like.

Chai is the word for "tea" in India, and it is often found brewed with a mixture of aromatic spices and sweetened hot milk, as in this recipe. If you like, you can also serve this chai over ice on a hot day. The peppercorns may seem like an odd addition to a drink, but they add a faint spicy heat and complexity to the mix.

The Middle East & North Africa

Cumin-Scented Falafel 47

Spiced Red Lentil Soup 48

Glazed Carrots with Coriander 49

Butternut Squash Tagine 50

Grilled Salmon with Chermoula 53

Moroccan-Spiced Chicken Skewers 54

Turkish-Style Meat Kabobs 56

Spiced Couscous with Apricots 57

Pistachio-Walnut Baklava 58

1½ cups (10½ oz/330 g) dried chickpeas
1 yellow onion, chopped
3 cloves garlic, chopped
1 cup (1 oz/30 g) packed fresh flat-leaf parsley leaves

1 tsp baking powder
1 tsp ground cumin
Salt
½ tsp chile flakes
Olive oil

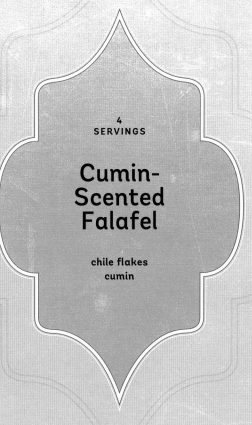

4
SERVINGS

Cumin-Scented Falafel

chile flakes
cumin

Bring a pot of lightly salted water to a boil. Add chickpeas and cook until slightly softened but still firm in center, 15–20 minutes. Drain chickpeas and cool slightly.

In a food processor, combine chickpeas with onion, garlic, and parsley and process until coarsely puréed. Transfer mixture to a bowl and stir in baking powder, cumin, ¾ teaspoon salt, and chile flakes. Refrigerate until cold, about 1 hour.

Pour a thin film of oil into a large nonstick frying pan over medium-high heat. With wet hands, shape small handfuls of chickpea mixture into patties about 3 inches (7.5 cm) across. You should have 12–14 patties.

Place 3 or 4 patties at a time in pan and cook, turning once, until browned on both sides, 4–6 minutes total. Repeat to shape and cook remaining falafel, adding more oil to pan as needed. Serve right away.

The musky flavor of cumin shines in these simple vegetarian patties. The secret to their satisfying texture is to use partially cooked chickpeas, form them into patties, and then quickly panfry them in hot oil. If you like, tuck the falafel into pita halves with diced tomatoes, prepared tahini sauce, and chopped lettuce.

4 SERVINGS

Spiced Red Lentil Soup

chile flakes
coriander
cumin
peppercorns

3 Tbsp olive oil

1 medium yellow onion, chopped

1 small yellow onion, halved and thinly sliced

1 tsp ground cumin

½ tsp ground coriander

Pinch of chile flakes

1 cup (7 oz/220 g) split red lentils, rinsed

1 carrot, peeled and finely chopped

1 ripe tomato, peeled, seeded, and chopped

4 cups (32 fl oz/1 l) vegetable broth

Salt and freshly ground black peppercorns

Juice from ½ lemon

Lemon wedges for serving

A trio of spices often found in the cuisine of Egypt—cumin, coriander, and chile flakes—flavors this easy-to-prepare soup. Keep lentils on hand in the pantry and you can make this healthy and satisfying soup any day of the week. Serve with a salad and crusty bread for a complete vegetarian meal.

In a small Dutch oven, heat 2 tablespoons of oil over medium-high heat. Add chopped onion and sauté until soft, about 5 minutes. Add cumin, coriander, and chile flakes and cook, stirring constantly, until spices are fragrant, about 30 seconds.

Add lentils, carrot, tomato, broth, 1 teaspoon salt, and 4 or 5 grinds of black pepper. Bring to a boil, reduce heat to medium, cover, and simmer, until the lentils fall apart and carrots are soft, about 40 minutes. Remove from heat and let cool for 15 minutes.

While soup is cooking, in a frying pan, heat remaining 1 tablespoon oil over medium heat. Add sliced onion and fry until browned and crisp on edges, about 15 minutes. Transfer to a plate.

In a blender or food processor, working in batches, process soup until a smooth purée forms. Return soup to pot, add lemon juice, and reheat over medium heat, stirring occasionally to prevent scorching.

Ladle soup into warmed bowls. Garnish with fried onion, and serve right away, accompanied by lemon wedges.

2 lb (1 kg) carrots, preferably a mixture of colors

1 tsp coriander seeds

¼ cup (2 oz/60 g) unsalted butter

½ lemon

3 Tbsp honey

Salt and freshly ground black peppercorns

2 Tbsp coarsely chopped fresh cilantro

Glazed Carrots with Coriander

**coriander
peppercorns**

Peel carrots, then cut on diagonal into slices ¼ inch (6 mm) thick.

In a small frying pan, toast coriander seeds over medium heat, shaking pan occasionally, until seeds are a shade darker and fragrant, about 2 minutes. Remove pan from heat and transfer seeds to a spice grinder or mortar and pestle and grind to a fine powder.

In a frying pan, melt butter over medium heat. Add ground coriander and cook, stirring occasionally, until fragrant, about 1 minute. Squeeze juice from lemon half into pan, add honey and ⅔ cup (5 fl oz/160 ml) water, and sauté for 1 minute. Add carrots, a pinch each of salt and pepper, and stir well. Raise heat to medium-high and cook, stirring occasionally, until carrots are just tender and liquid is reduced to a glaze, 12–15 minutes. If carrots are still not tender after liquid has reduced, add a bit more water to pan and continue to cook.

Stir cilantro into carrots, then taste and adjust seasonings. Transfer to a warmed serving dish and serve right away.

Coriander is in the same botanical family as carrots, so it makes sense that the two go so well together. Moroccan cooks often pair the duo in the fresh salads of the region, which inspired this new twist on a classic French side dish. Reinforce the lemony flavor of the coriander seeds with a sprinkle of chopped fresh cilantro just before serving.

6 SERVINGS

Butternut Squash Tagine

cinnamon
ginger
peppercorns
turmeric

2 Tbsp olive oil

1 large yellow onion, finely chopped

1 tsp ground ginger

½ tsp ground cinnamon

½ tsp ground turmeric

1 butternut squash, peeled, seeded, and cubed

1 large carrot, peeled and sliced on diagonal

1 large tomato, seeded and chopped

3 Tbsp dried currants

1 Tbsp honey

Salt and freshly ground black peppercorns

1 large sweet potato

This fragrant Moroccan-style stew pairs autumn vegetables with an aromatic trio of spices typical to the region. North American cooks usually use cinnamon and ginger in sweet dishes, but, as this dish shows, the spices also contribute to complex and fragrant savory preparations in the cuisine of North Africa.

In a tagine or Dutch oven, heat oil over medium-high heat. Add onion and cook, stirring often, until softened, about 5 minutes. Stir in ginger, cinnamon, and turmeric and cook, stirring often, until spices are fragrant, about 30 seconds. Add squash, carrot, tomato, currants, honey, and ¾ cup (6 fl oz/180 ml) water. Season to taste with salt and pepper. Bring to a boil, reduce heat to medium, cover, and simmer for 10 minutes.

Peel sweet potato, cut in half lengthwise, and then cut each half into large chunks. Add to pot, re-cover, and cook until vegetables are tender but still hold their shape, about 25 minutes.

Serve right away, directly from pot. Or let cool, cover, and refrigerate for up to 2 days and reheat gently before serving.

3 Tbsp fresh lemon juice

1/3 cup (1/3 oz/10 g) fresh flat-leaf parsley

1/3 cup (1/3 oz/10 g) fresh cilantro

1 Tbsp minced preserved lemon

1 1/2 tsp Spanish smoked paprika

3/4 tsp ground cumin

1 clove garlic, coarsely chopped

Salt

5 Tbsp (3 fl oz/80 ml) olive oil

4–6 salmon fillets, about 6 oz (185 g) each

Grilled Salmon with Chermoula

cumin
smoked paprika

In a mortar, combine lemon juice, parsley, cilantro, preserved lemon, paprika, cumin, garlic, and 1/4 teaspoon salt. Using a pestle, and working in a circular motion, grind the ingredients together to a thick paste. This can take a few minutes. Slowly drizzle in oil while stirring constantly with pestle until a smooth mixture forms. (Alternatively, in a blender or food processer, combine oil, lemon juice, parsley, cilantro, preserved lemon, paprika, cumin, garlic, and 1/4 teaspoon salt and process until smooth.) Place half of mixture in a shallow bowl large enough to hold fish, reserving other half. Place fish in bowl and turn to coat with marinade. Cover and refrigerate for at least 30 minutes or up to 1 hour.

Prepare a grill for direct grilling over medium-high heat. Brush and generously oil grill rack.

Place salmon on grill rack directly over hot coals or heating elements. Grill, carefully turning once with a wide spatula, until fish is opaque but still looks moist in center when tested with a knife, 6–10 minutes.

Transfer fish to a warmed platter, brush with reserved herb mixture, and serve right away.

Chermoula is a classic spice-and-herb sauce from Morocco and surrounding countries that is often used as a marinade and sauce for seafood. This version has a Spanish influence, complementing cumin's slightly smoky taste with smoked paprika. For a full meal, serve with steamed couscous.

4 SERVINGS

Moroccan-Spiced Chicken Skewers

cayenne
cinnamon
cumin
garlic powder
sweet paprika
turmeric

1 tsp ground cumin
1 tsp sweet paprika
1 tsp ground turmeric
½ tsp ground cinnamon
¼ tsp garlic powder
⅛ tsp cayenne pepper
Salt
1¼ lb (625 g) skinless, boneless chicken breasts, cubed

2 Tbsp olive oil
1 large red bell pepper, seeded and cut into 8 pieces
1 cup (6 oz/185 g) instant couscous
2 Tbsp chopped fresh cilantro

As with the curry masalas of India, home cooks in North Africa blend their own unique mixture of spices for their personal recipes. This one highlights the use of cinnamon in savory dishes to add complexity. Quickly cooked and served with a simple herbed couscous, these skewers are achievable any day of the week.

Prepare a grill for direct grilling over high heat. While grill heats, soak 4 bamboo skewers in water to cover. Brush grill rack generously with oil.

In a small bowl, stir together cumin, paprika, turmeric, cinnamon, garlic powder, cayenne, and 1 teaspoon salt. In a large bowl, toss chicken with oil to coat. Sprinkle with spice mixture and toss again to coat. Drain skewers. Thread chicken and bell pepper pieces onto skewers, dividing them evenly and pressing them together snugly. Place skewers on grill rack directly over hot coals or heat elements and cover. Grill, turning occasionally, until chicken is browned and feels firm when pressed, 8–10 minutes.

While chicken and peppers are grilling, in a small saucepan, combine 1½ cups (12 fl oz/375 ml) water and ½ teaspoon salt and bring to a boil over high heat. Stir in couscous and return to a boil. Cover tightly and remove from heat. Let stand until couscous absorbs water, about 5 minutes. Stir in cilantro. Serve right away with couscous.

Turkish-Style Meat Kebabs

cayenne
coriander
cumin
peppercorns

½ lb (250 g) ground lamb
½ lb (250 g) ground veal
1 tsp ground coriander
1 tsp ground cumin

¼ tsp cayenne pepper
Salt and freshly ground black peppercorns
1 lemon, cut into 4 wedges

These boldly spiced ground meat patties are based on *kofte*, a classic dish from Turkey. There, they are usually spicy, so feel free to add more cayenne pepper if you like your food on the hot side. Serve with grilled vegetables, or tuck them into warm pita bread rounds with sliced tomato and onion.

In large bowl, combine lamb, veal, coriander, cumin, cayenne, 1 teaspoon salt, and ¼ teaspoon black pepper and mix with a fork to combine. Cover and refrigerate for at least 6 hours or up to 24 hours.

Prepare a grill for direct grilling over medium-high heat, or preheat a stove-top grill pan over medium-high heat. If using a grill, brush and oil grill rack.

Divide meat mixture into 4 equal portions. On a work surface, using your hands, shape each portion into a patty 6 inches (15 cm) long and 2 inches (5 cm) wide. Insert a 12-inch (30-cm) metal skewer lengthwise down center of each patty, with its tip 1 inch (2.5 cm) above top edge of meat. Lift long edges of meat up and press them together, making a cylinder around skewer. Pinch to seal well.

Place kebabs on grill rack directly over hot coals or heat elements, or place in grill pan, and cook, turning with tongs as needed, until meat is no longer pink in center, about 8 minutes.

Serve right away with the lemon wedges for squeezing.

2/3 cup (3 oz/90 g) slivered almonds

2 Tbsp olive oil

2 cups (12 oz/375 g) instant couscous

1/3 cup (2 oz/60 g) dried apricot halves, cut into thin slivers

2 2/3 cups (21 fl oz/645 ml) chicken broth or water

1/2 tsp ground turmeric

Salt

1/4 cup dried currants

1 tsp finely grated orange zest

2 Tbsp fresh lemon juice

1/2 cup (3/4 oz) chopped fresh mint

Freshly ground black peppercorns

Spiced Couscous with Apricots

peppercorns
turmeric

Preheat oven to 350°F (180°C). Spread almonds in a single layer on a baking sheet and toast, stirring once or twice, until golden, 8–10 minutes. Immediately pour onto a plate to cool.

In a large bowl, drizzle olive oil over couscous and toss to coat thoroughly. Scatter apricots over couscous.

In a small saucepan, bring broth to a boil over medium-high heat. Stir in turmeric and 1/4 teaspoon salt, then pour broth mixture over couscous. Cover bowl tightly with foil and let stand until couscous is tender and liquid is absorbed, about 5 minutes.

Remove foil and fluff grains with a fork. Stir in about half of almonds and all of currants, orange zest, lemon juice, and mint. Season with pepper and taste and adjust seasoning.

Transfer couscous to a bowl and garnish with remaining almonds. Serve right away.

Turmeric is often mixed with other spices to create an aromatic blend for the highly spiced foods of the region. But it is also delicious on its own, and this recipe showcases the spice's unique, subtle flavor and bold yellow color. Serve this as an accompaniment to a tagine or stew or alongside roasted meats, poultry, or fish.

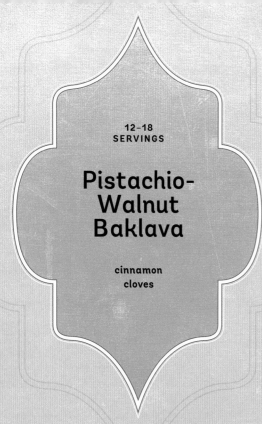

12–18 SERVINGS

Pistachio-Walnut Baklava

cinnamon
cloves

1½ cups (6 oz/185 g) shelled, unsalted, raw pistachios, plus 3 Tbsp chopped

1 cup (4 oz/125 g) walnuts

3 Tbsp plus ¾ cup (6 oz/185 g) sugar

1 tsp ground cinnamon

¼ tsp ground cloves

¼ tsp salt

1 lb (500 g) filo dough, thawed if frozen

½ cup (4 oz/125 g) unsalted butter, melted

1 cup (12 oz/375 g) honey

This popular Turkish dessert features a medley of ground cinnamon and cloves which, when mixed with honey, represent a characteristic flavor profile for desserts in that part of the world. Filo can be difficult to work with; be patient and keep the sheets covered while working and you'll learn how best to work with it.

In a food processor, combine 1½ cups (6 oz/185 g) pistachios, all walnuts, 3 tablespoons of sugar, cinnamon, cloves, and salt. Pulse until finely ground. Transfer to a bowl and set aside.

To assemble baklava, lay stack of filo sheets flat on a cutting board with long side of rectangle facing you. Cut stack of sheets in half vertically to make 2 rectangles, each roughly 8 by 12 inches (20 by 30 cm). Pile sheets in a single stack and cover with a sheet of plastic wrap, then a dampened kitchen towel.

Brush a 9-by-13-inch (23-by-33-cm) baking dish with melted butter. Place 1 sheet of filo in dish and brush it lightly with melted butter, working from edges to center. Repeat to make 12 layers. Sprinkle about one-fourth of nut mixture evenly over top sheet, then top with 2 more buttered filo sheets. Sprinkle on another one-fourth of nut mixture, followed by 2 more buttered filo sheets. Repeat once more, then finish with remaining one-fourth of nut mixture and all of remaining filo (about 12 sheets), again brushing each sheet with butter. Brush top sheet generously with remaining butter and refrigerate dish for 15 minutes.

Preheat oven to 350°F (180°C).

Using a thin, serrated knife, cut baklava into 18 rectangles (3 across short side and 6 across long side), and then cut each rectangle into 2 triangles. Bake until golden brown, 50 minutes to 1 hour. Transfer to a wire rack and let cool slightly.

In a small saucepan, combine remaining ¾ cup (6 oz/185 g) sugar and ½ cup (4 fl oz/125 ml) water and bring to a boil over medium heat, stirring to dissolve sugar. Boil, without stirring, until mixture registers 220°F (105°C) on a candy thermometer, about 5 minutes. Remove from heat and stir in honey.

Pour syrup evenly over warm baklava (be careful, as mixture may splatter). Sprinkle top with 3 tablespoons chopped pistachios. Cover loosely with waxed paper and let stand at room temperature for at least 8 hours or up to overnight.

To serve, run a knife along cuts, then remove pieces from dish with a thin metal spatula. Layer leftover pieces in an airtight container, separating layers with waxed paper, and store at room temperature for up to 1 week.

Both Greece and Turkey claim this spiced, nut-filled pastry as their own, but it can be seen throughout the Mediterranean region. Freshly made filo pastry can be found in Middle Eastern markets. Packages of frozen filo can be found in many supermarkets. Follow the instructions on the package to thaw frozen filo before using.

Europe

Roasted Vegetables
with Romesco 63

Bucatini all'Arrabbiata 64

Spinach & Three-Cheese Lasagne 65

Pizza with Fennel Sausage
& Peppers 66

Hungarian-Style
Paprika Chicken 69

Braised Sauerkraut
& Sausages 70

Red Cabbage with Apples
& Juniper 71

Swedish Cardamom Twist 72

Honey-Spice Cake 74

3 cloves garlic, 1 whole and 2 smashed

½ cup (2½ oz/75 g) slivered almonds, toasted

1 jar (12 oz/375 g) roasted red bell peppers, drained

2 tsp sherry vinegar

1 tsp Spanish smoked paprika

3 Tbsp plus ¼ cup (2 fl oz/60 ml) olive oil

Salt and freshly ground black peppercorns

1 lb (500 g) small red-skinned potatoes, halved

2 large zucchini, cut into thick slices

2 Asian eggplants, cut into thick slices

1 large red bell pepper, seeded and cut into thick slices

1 red onion, cut into wedges

4–6
SERVINGS

Roasted Vegetables with Romesco

peppercorns
smoked paprika

Preheat oven to 450°F (230°C). To make romesco, in a food processor, chop whole garlic clove finely. Add almonds and pulse until finely chopped. Add roasted bell peppers, vinegar, and paprika and process until smooth. With machine running, gradually add 3 tablespoons of oil. Season with salt and pepper. Set aside.

In a small saucepan, heat ¼ cup (2 fl oz/60 ml) oil and crushed garlic cloves over medium-low heat until garlic is golden, about 5 minutes. Remove from heat and discard garlic. On a large, rimmed baking sheet, toss potatoes with 1 tablespoon of garlic oil and roast for 10 minutes.

In a large bowl, toss zucchini, eggplant, chopped bell pepper, and onion with remaining garlic oil and add to baking sheet with potatoes. Roast, turning occasionally, until vegetables are tender, 20–30 minutes. Season with salt and pepper. Transfer vegetables to a platter. Put romesco sauce in small bowl for dipping and place on platter. Serve right away.

Romesco is a classic Spanish sauce made from red bell peppers, almonds, and olive oil, which are all native to the country. This version is bolstered with another regional product, smoked paprika, which echoes the smoky flavor of the roasted peppers. The sauce is equally delicious alongside roasted poultry or meat.

4–6 SERVINGS

Bucatini all'Arrabbiata

chile flakes
peppercorns

The zesty sauce featured here is so named because it includes a generous measure of fiery chile flakes (*arrabbiata* means "angry" in Italian). Bucatini, long, thin, hollow pasta strands, are traditional, but you could use any type of dried pasta that you have on hand. Top with freshly grated Parmesan cheese, if you like.

1 can (28 oz/875 g) plum tomatoes, drained

6 Tbsp (3 fl oz/90 ml) olive oil

4 large cloves garlic, minced

1 small yellow onion, minced

¼–½ tsp chile flakes, or to taste

2 Tbsp tomato paste

Salt

3 Tbsp minced fresh flat-leaf parsley

Salt and freshly ground black peppercorns

1 lb (500 g) bucatini

Using your fingers, push out the excess seeds from tomatoes and place tomatoes in a bowl. With your hands, a fork, or a potato masher, crush tomatoes well.

In a frying pan large enough to accommodate the pasta later, warm 4 tablespoons (2 fl oz/60 ml) of olive oil over medium-low heat. Add garlic, onion, and chile flakes and heat gently, stirring occasionally, until onion is translucent, about 4 minutes. Stir in tomato paste, add crushed tomatoes and ½ teaspoon salt, and stir again. Simmer gently until sauce is thickened, about 20 minutes. Remove from heat and stir in parsley and remaining 2 tablespoons olive oil. Taste and adjust the seasoning, then cover and keep warm.

While sauce is simmering, cook bucatini in a large pot of rapidly boiling salted water, stirring occasionally, until al dente, according to package directions.

Drain pasta, add to sauce in frying pan, and toss until strands are well coated with sauce. Serve right away.

Salt

2 lb (1 kg) fresh spinach, tough stems removed

1 lb (500 g) ricotta cheese

¼ cup (1½ oz/45 g) minced shallots

2 Tbsp fresh thyme leaves

1 large egg

¼ cup (2 oz/60 g) butter

¼ cup (1½ oz/45 g) all-purpose flour

¼ tsp freshly grated nutmeg

⅛ tsp cayenne pepper

3 cups (24 fl oz/750 ml) whole milk, heated

1 box (7 oz/220 g) no-boil lasagne noodles (16 noodles)

6 oz (185 g) *pecorino romano* cheese, grated

10 oz (315 g) fresh mozzarella cheese, thinly sliced

6 SERVINGS

Spinach & Three-Cheese Lasagne

cayenne
nutmeg

Add 1 teaspoon salt and spinach to large pot of boiling water and cook until spinach is tender but still bright green, 4–6 minutes. Drain and rinse under running cold water. Squeeze dry and chop coarsely. Squeeze dry again and set aside.

In a bowl, mix together ricotta, shallots, thyme, egg, and ½ teaspoon salt. Set aside. In a saucepan over medium heat, melt butter. Whisk in flour, ½ teaspoon salt, nutmeg, and cayenne until a paste forms. Slowly whisk in hot milk, reduce heat to medium-low, and cook, whisking often, until sauce is thickened, about 15 minutes. Remove from heat.

Preheat oven to 375°F (190°C). Pour a thin layer of sauce in bottom of a 9-by-13-inch (23-by-33-cm) baking dish. Add 4 lasagne noodles. Top with one-third of spinach, a thin layer of sauce, one-third of ricotta mixture, one-third of *pecorino romano*, and one-fourth of mozzarella. Repeat the layers twice, then top with the remaining 4 noodles. Pour over remaining sauce. Top with the remaining slices of mozzarella. Bake until sauce is bubbling, top is brown, and pasta is tender to the bite, about 45 minutes. Let stand for 10 minutes. Cut into squares and serve right away.

In North America, nutmeg is known as a spice for desserts, but in classical French and Italian cooking, it is often added to white sauces or dishes that feature spinach to lend a nutty complexity. Here, it is coupled with cayenne pepper to flavor an easy lasagne made with no-boil noodles and a trio of Italian-style cheeses.

Pizza with Fennel Sausage & Peppers

chile flakes
coriander
fennel seeds
peppercorns

½ tsp fennel seeds

½ tsp ground coriander

Salt and freshly ground black peppercorns

Pinch plus ¼ tsp chile flakes

½ lb (250 g) ground pork

2 tsp plus 1 Tbsp olive oil

Cornmeal for dusting

1 lb (500 g) purchased pizza dough

½ cup (2 oz/60 g) shredded mozzarella cheese

1 large jarred roasted red bell pepper, seeded and thinly sliced

It's easy to make your own Italian-style sausage at home using ground pork, preferably freshly ground shoulder from the butcher. This version features lemony coriander, aniselike fennel seeds, and spicy chile flakes on a homemade pizza. You can also form the mixture into patties and fry them for a weekend brunch.

To make sausage, in a mini food processor, combine fennel seeds, coriander, 1 teaspoon salt, ½ teaspoon black pepper, and pinch of chile flakes. Process to a paste. Transfer seasoning mixture to a bowl and add ground pork; mix with a fork. Refrigerate for 1 hour to blend the flavors.

Place a rack in lowest position in oven and preheat to 400°F (200°C). Grease a baking sheet or 12-inch (30-cm) pizza pan with 2 teaspoons oil and dust with cornmeal. On a lightly floured work surface, pat and stretch dough into a 12-inch (30-cm) round. Transfer to prepared baking sheet and set aside.

Heat 1 tablespoon oil in a frying pan over medium heat. Add sausage, breaking it into small pieces with your fingers, and cook, stirring gently, until lightly browned on all sides, 8–10 minutes. Transfer to a paper towel–lined plate to drain.

Scatter cheese, roasted pepper, and sausage evenly on top of dough. Sprinkle with ¼ teaspoon chile flakes. Bake until crust is golden brown on edges and cheese is bubbling, 15–18 minutes. Let cool slightly, then cut into squares or wedges and serve right away.

Hungarian-Style Paprika Chicken

**peppercorns
sweet paprika**

1 chicken, 3–4 lb (1.5–2 kg), cut into 8 pieces

Salt and freshly ground black peppercorns

2 Tbsp unsalted butter

2 Tbsp canola oil

2 yellow onions, finely chopped

1 green bell pepper, seeded and finely chopped

½ cup (4 fl oz/125 ml) low-sodium chicken broth

2 Tbsp sweet paprika

2 tomatoes, seeded and chopped

½ cup (4 oz/125 g) sour cream

Season chicken all over with salt and pepper. In a Dutch oven, melt butter with oil over medium-high heat. Working in batches, add chicken and cook, turning frequently, until browned, about 10 minutes per batch. Remove from pan and set aside.

Pour off all but 1 tablespoon of fat in pot. Add onions and bell pepper and sauté over medium-high heat until softened, about 5 minutes. Stir in broth, paprika, and tomatoes and deglaze pan, stirring and scraping up browned bits on bottom of pan with a wooden spoon.

Add tomato mixture, cover pot, and cook over medium heat until chicken is tender and opaque throughout, about 45 minutes. Transfer chicken to a platter and cover loosely with aluminum foil to keep warm. Bring cooking liquid to a boil over high heat and cook, uncovered, until slightly thickened, about 2 minutes. Remove from heat, stir in sour cream, and season to taste with salt and pepper. Serve right away.

Hungarian cooks use their native paprika to flavor a variety of dishes, such as this savory chicken stew. You'll often see Hungarian-style stews and goulashes made with sour cream, which helps carry the flavors of the spice while mellowing it slightly. Serve this over buttered egg noodles to enjoy with the sauce.

Braised Sauerkraut & Sausages

cloves
juniper berries
peppercorns

3 lb (1.5 kg) prepared sauerkraut

1 clove garlic, smashed

10 juniper berries

1 bay leaf

2 whole cloves

6 black peppercorns

¼ cup (2 oz/60 g) canola oil

1 large yellow onion, minced

4 smoked ham hocks, about 2 lb (1 kg) total weight

2 cups (16 fl oz/500 ml) dry white wine

Freshly ground black peppercorns

8 red-skinned potatoes, about 3 lb (1.5 kg) total weight

6 pork or chicken sausages

Juniper berries are a common addition to German-style cooking and to the cuisine of Alsace in France, whose dishes are heavily influenced by the neighboring country. Here, juniper adds woodsy flavor to a classic sausage and sauerkraut combination known there as *choucroute garni*. Cloves and peppercorns add complexity.

Preheat oven to 325°F (165°C).

Drain sauerkraut, place in a kitchen towel, gather up ends, and wring out any excess water. Tie garlic, juniper berries, bay leaf, cloves, and peppercorns in a small square of cheesecloth.

In a Dutch oven, warm oil over medium heat. Add onion and sauté until translucent but not browned, about 5 minutes. Add half of sauerkraut, cheesecloth bundle, and ham hocks and top with remaining sauerkraut. Add wine, ½ teaspoon black pepper, and water to nearly cover and bring to a boil. Cover, transfer to oven, and cook for 1 hour. Stir the mixture, re-cover and cook for 1 hour longer.

Remove from oven, stir, and place potatoes on top. Re-cover and cook until potatoes are tender when pierced with a fork, about 30 minutes. Meanwhile, bring a saucepan full of water to a boil over high heat. Add sausages, reduce heat to medium, and cook until hot, 6–8 minutes. Discard cheesecloth bundle.

Using a slotted spoon, transfer to a warmed, deep platter and top with ham hocks and sausages. Surround sauerkraut and meat with potatoes. Serve right away.

Red Cabbage with Apples & Juniper

**juniper berries
peppercorns**

1 head red cabbage, about ¾ lb (375 g)

4 Granny Smith apples

3 Tbsp unsalted butter

1 red onion, minced

3 juniper berries

¼ cup (2 fl oz/60 ml) red wine vinegar

¼ cup (2 fl oz/60 ml) low-sodium chicken broth

Salt and ½ tsp freshly ground black peppercorns

Cut cabbage in half, remove and discard core, and slice thinly. Halve and core 2 apples (leave them unpeeled), then cut into 1-inch (2.5-cm) cubes.

In a heavy saucepan over medium heat, melt butter. Add onion and sauté until translucent, 2–3 minutes. Add cubed apples and sauté until slightly softened, 3–4 minutes. Add cabbage and juniper berries and sauté until cabbage is glistening and color has lightened, 5–6 minutes. Add vinegar and deglaze pan, stirring and scraping up browned bits on bottom of pan with a wooden spoon. Add broth, ½ teaspoon salt, and ½ teaspoon black pepper and bring to a boil. Reduce heat to low, cover, and simmer until cabbage is pale pink and tender, about 15 minutes.

Meanwhile, peel, halve, and core remaining 2 apples, then shred using large holes of a grater-shredder. When cabbage is done, remove from heat and stir in shredded apple. Serve right away.

Juniper berries are often used to flavor meats and cabbage braised in red wine in Germany and Austria. This dish, influenced by the cuisine of the region, serves as the perfect backdrop for juniper's piney aroma and floral nuances. Grated fresh apple stirred in at the end keeps the dish tasting fresh.

1 LOAF

Swedish Cardamom Twist

cardamom
cinnamon

10 cardamom pods
½ cup (4 fl oz/125 ml) whole milk
½ cup (4 oz/125 g) unsalted butter, at room temperature
2½–3 cups (12½–15 oz/ 390–465 g) bread flour

¼ tsp salt
½ cup (4 oz/125 g) sugar
1 package (2¼ tsp) quick-rise yeast
Canola oil for bowl
1 tsp ground cinnamon
1 large egg yolk beaten with 1 tsp water

Cardamom is to Swedish baked goods what cinnamon is to desserts in North America. In Sweden, you see cardamom in nearly every sugary treat. Here, the spice is kneaded into a sweet yeast dough braided around a cinnamon-flecked filling. Serve it as part of a company brunch.

Gently crack cardamom pods with side of a chef's knife. Remove seeds and discard pods. In a mortar, spice grinder, or coffee mill reserved for spices, Crush with a pestle or grind to a coarse powder.

In a saucepan, combine ½ cup (4 fl oz/125 ml) water, milk, ¼ cup (2 oz/60 g) of butter, and cardamom seeds over low heat. Heat until warm (105°–115°F/40°–46°C).

In a bowl, combine 1 cup (5 oz/155 g) of flour, salt, ¼ cup (2 oz/60 g) of sugar, and yeast. Using a spoon, beat in warm milk mixture until smooth. Gradually beat in 1½ cups (7½ oz/ 235 g) more flour to make a soft dough that holds its shape. Turn dough out onto a lightly floured work surface and knead, adding remaining flour as needed, until smooth and elastic, about 10 minutes.

Form dough into a ball, transfer to a lightly oiled bowl, turn to coat with oil, and cover bowl with plastic wrap. Let dough rise in a warm, draft-free spot until it doubles in bulk, 1½–2 hours.

Meanwhile, in a small bowl, cream together remaining ¼ cup butter, remaining ¼ cup sugar, and cinnamon.

Dust a rimmed baking sheet with flour. Punch down dough and turn out onto a lightly floured surface. Form into a ball and knead until smooth, about 1 minute. Let rest for 10 minutes. Roll out dough into a 9-by-12-inch (23-by-30-cm) rectangle.

Spread filling evenly over dough, leaving a 1-inch (2.5-cm) border uncovered on all sides. Starting at long side farthest from you, roll up rectangle toward you into a log. Place roll, seam side down, on baking sheet.

Using scissors and cutting at an angle, snip roll at ½-inch (12-mm) intervals, cutting almost halfway through. Pull and push snipped sections of dough alternately to left and right, twisting each section slightly to expose filling inside. Cover loosely with a kitchen towel and let rise in a warm, draft-free spot until it doubles in size, about 1 hour.

Preheat oven to 375°F (190°C). Brush loaf with yolk mixture. Bake bread until golden brown, 25–30 minutes. Let cool on a wire rack. Cut into slices with a serrated knife to serve. Store leftovers in an airtight container at room temperature for up to 2 days.

Whole cardamom is available in green or white pods, but many believe cardamom from green pods to have superior flavor. Like many spices, cardamom's flavor dissipates quickly. It's best to buy whole pods, then crush them to infuse into liquids, or shake out the seeds and grind them just before using in recipes.

8–10 SERVINGS

Honey-Spice Cake

allspice
cayenne
cinnamon
coriander

2 cups (10 oz/315 g) all-purpose flour

2 tsp baking powder

¾ tsp ground coriander

¾ tsp ground allspice

½ tsp salt

½ tsp ground cinnamon

¼ tsp cayenne pepper

¾ cup (6 fl oz/170 ml) whole milk, at room temperature

1 tsp vanilla extract

¾ cup (6 oz/180 g) plus 1 Tbsp unsalted butter, at room temperature

1 cup (7 oz/220 g) firmly packed brown sugar

½ cup (4 oz/125 g) plus 2 Tbsp granulated sugar

2 large eggs, at room temperature, lightly beaten

½ cup (3 oz/90 g) golden raisins

¼ cup (3 oz/90 g) honey

This recipe is based on French-style *pain d'epices*, which is made from a blend of fragrant spices and honey. Though not traditional, this cake features a small measure of cayenne pepper for a pleasing kick that helps bring the other flavors into focus. It keeps well, so you can make it ahead and store it, tightly wrapped, for a few days.

Preheat oven to 350°F (180°C). Line bottom of a 9-inch (23-cm) round cake pan with parchment paper.

Sift flour, baking powder, coriander, allspice, salt, cinnamon, and cayenne together onto a sheet of parchment paper; set aside. In a small bowl, combine milk and vanilla; set aside.

Using a stand mixer, beat ¾ cup (6 oz/185 g) butter with paddle on medium speed until creamy. Add brown sugar and ½ cup (4 oz/125 g) granulated sugar and beat until mixture is pale and fluffy. Slowly add eggs, beating each until incorporated before continuing. Reduce speed to medium-low and add dry ingredients in 3 additions alternately with milk mixture in 2 additions, starting and ending with dry ingredients. Beat just until combined. Fold in raisins.

Pour batter into prepared pan and smooth top. Bake until cake is browned and puffed and a skewer inserted into center comes out clean, 35–40 minutes. Let cool completely on a wire rack. Run a knife around edge of pan and invert cake onto rack. Peel off parchment paper and turn cake right side up on a plate.

In a small saucepan, combine 2 tablespoons granulated sugar, honey, and 1 tablespoon butter. Bring to a boil over medium heat, stirring constantly, and cook for about 3 minutes to make a glaze. Pour over cake. With an offset spatula, smooth glaze on top and sides. Cut into wedges to serve.

Latin America & The Caribbean

Latin-Style Black Bean Soup 79

Cuban-Style Red Beans & Rice 80

Grilled Chile-Lime Corn 81

Spice-Crusted Fish Tacos 82

Chicken Fajitas with Cabbage Slaw 84

Caribbean-Style Jerk Chicken 85

Grilled Skirt Steak
with Chimichurri 87

Cinnamon-Sugar Churros 88

Chocolate-Ancho
Chile Cake 90

3 cups (21 oz/655 g) dried black beans

1 bay leaf

1 smoked ham hock, about 1 lb (500 g)

2 Tbsp olive oil

2 yellow onions, chopped

1 red bell pepper, seeded and chopped

4 cloves garlic, minced

1 Tbsp ground cumin

1 tsp dried oregano

½ tsp ground cinnamon

⅛ tsp ground cloves

2–3 Tbsp fresh lime juice

1 tsp hot red pepper sauce, or more to taste

Salt and freshly ground black peppercorns

Chopped fresh cilantro, chopped red onion, and sour cream for serving

8 SERVINGS

Latin-Style Black Bean Soup

cinnamon
cloves
cumin
peppercorns

Pick over beans and discard any misshapen beans or stones. Rinse beans under running cold water, drain, and place in a saucepan. Add water to cover and bring to a boil over high heat. Boil for 2 minutes, then remove beans from heat, cover, and let stand for 1 hour.

Drain beans and return to saucepan. Add 8 cups (64 fl oz/2 l) water, bay leaf, and ham hock. Bring to a boil over high heat. Cover partially, reduce heat to low, and simmer.

Meanwhile, in a large frying pan, heat oil over medium heat. Add onions and bell pepper and sauté, stirring occasionally, until vegetables are tender and onions are translucent, about 10 minutes. Add garlic, cumin, oregano, cinnamon, and cloves and cook about 2 minutes longer. Add onion mixture to beans and simmer until very tender, 1–1½ hours; timing will depend upon age of beans.

Remove soup from heat. Remove ham hock and set aside for another use (see note). Remove bay leaf and discard. Working in batches, purée half of the soup in a blender. Return soup to a saucepan with unpuréed mixture and season with lime juice, hot pepper sauce, ½ teaspoon salt, and ¼ teaspoon pepper. Gradually reheat over medium heat, stirring often to prevent scorching. Taste and adjust seasonings.

Ladle soup into warmed individual bowls. Top each serving with cilantro, red onion, and sour cream and serve right away.

This vibrant soup is influenced by the cuisine of Mexico's Oaxaca state, which is famous for mole, ground mixtures of spices, seeds, and nuts that form the basis for a variety of soups and stews. For a heartier soup, remove the ham meat from the bone, shred it with your fingers, and stir it back into the hot soup.

6 SERVINGS

Cuban-Style Red Beans & Rice

cumin
peppercorns

Cumin is popular around the world. In Latin America and Cuba, you often find it in bean dishes such as this one, which are a staple of the region. You can also prepare this dish with black beans. Serve it alongside Latin-inspired seafood, poultry, or meat dishes.

1 cup (7 oz/220 g) dried red beans

1 bay leaf

Salt and freshly ground black peppercorns

2 tsp olive oil

3 strips thick-sliced bacon, chopped

½ white onion, chopped

1 green or red bell pepper, seeded and chopped

2 cloves garlic, minced

2 tsp dried oregano

2 tsp ground cumin

1 can (8 fl oz/250 ml) tomato sauce

1½ cups (10½ oz/330 g) uncooked long-grain white rice

2½ cups (20 fl oz/625 ml) chicken broth or water

Pick over beans and discard any misshapen beans or stones. Rinse beans under running cold water, drain, and place in a saucepan. Add water to cover and bring to a boil over high heat. Boil for 2 minutes, then remove beans from heat, cover, and let stand for 1 hour.

Drain beans and return to saucepan. Add 8 cups (64 fl oz/2 l) water and bay leaf and bring to a boil over high heat. Reduce heat to low and simmer for 1 hour. Add 1 teaspoon salt and simmer until beans are very tender but not cracked, 2–3 hours. Remove from heat and let beans cool in their liquid.

In a sauté pan with a lid, heat oil over medium heat. Add bacon and sauté until browned and crisp, about 8 minutes. Add onion, bell pepper, and garlic and sauté until vegetables are softened, about 2 minutes. Add oregano, cumin, and ½ teaspoon black pepper and cook until fragrant, about 1 minute. Add tomato sauce and cook until most of liquid has evaporated, about 5 minutes. Add rice, stir to coat with tomato mixture, and sauté until rice has absorbed tomato sauce. Add broth, stir once, and bring to a boil. Reduce heat to low, cover, and cook until rice has absorbed all of liquid, about 20 minutes.

Using a large spoon, transfer beans, along with a few spoonfuls of cooking liquid, to pan with rice and stir in. Cover and cook until rice has absorbed all liquid, about 10 minutes. Remove from heat and let stand, covered, for 5 minutes, then stir gently. Season to taste with salt. Serve right away.

6 ears corn, unshucked

2 limes, quartered

Mexican *crema* or sour cream

Crumbled cotija or freshly grated Parmesan cheese

Ancho or New Mexico chile powder

Cayenne pepper (optional)

Salt

Grilled Chile-Lime Corn

cayenne
chile powder

Carefully pull back the husks from the corn, remove the silk, and put the husks back in place. Soak the ears in cold water to cover for 30 minutes.

Prepare a grill for direct-heat cooking over high heat. Generously oil the grill rack.

Remove corn from water and place it directly over hot coals or heating elements. Grill, turning frequently, until corn is tender, about 20 minutes. If husk is burned but corn is not yet tender, wrap in foil and continue to cook until done.

To serve, pull back husk on corn ears. Rub corn with lime quarters, drizzle with *crema*, and sprinkle with cheese, chile powder, cayenne, if you like it hot, and season to taste with salt. Serve right away.

During summer grilling season, when corn appears in the market, bring some home and cook it as the Mexicans do, sprinkled to taste with lime juice, *crema* (the Mexican version of sour cream), cheese, chile powder, and salt. If you like, set out extra lime quarters for squeezing over the sweet corn.

4 SERVINGS

Spice-Crusted Fish Tacos

chile powder
cumin

Fish tacos abound in countries all over the Latin and Caribbean region. This version features a mixture of cumin and chile powder that, when mixed with oil, doubles as a spice rub and a marinade to perk up mild white fish. Try rock cod, rockfish, or snapper fillets and make sure your grill rack is well oiled to prevent sticking.

4 mild white fish fillets, 6–8 oz (185–250 g) each

¼ cup (2 fl oz/60 ml) canola oil, plus more for greasing

½ tsp ground cumin

½ tsp ancho or New Mexico chile powder

8 corn tortillas

1 ripe avocado

2 cloves garlic, minced

¼ cup (⅓ oz/10 g) chopped fresh cilantro

2 Tbsp fresh lime juice

Hot red pepper sauce

Salt

1 *each* red and yellow bell pepper, halved lengthwise and seeded

Fresh tomato salsa

Fresh cilantro leaves and lime wedges for serving

Prepare a grill for direct-heat cooking over medium-high heat.

Place fillets in a glass or ceramic dish just large enough to hold them. In a small bowl, combine oil, cumin, and chile powder. Pour over fish and turn to coat evenly on both sides. Let stand at room temperature for about 30 minutes.

Wrap tortillas in aluminum foil and place on edge of grill rack and heat for about 10 minutes on each side.

Meanwhile, peel and pit the avocado and then cut it into cubes. In a bowl, combine avocado cubes, garlic, cilantro, lime juice, and hot pepper sauce and salt to taste and mix gently. Cover bowl with plastic wrap and set aside.

Generously oil grill rack. Place peppers and fish fillets on grill rack directly over the hot coals or heating elements and cook peppers until softened and lightly browned, 4–5 minutes. Cook fillets, turning once, until lightly browned and opaque throughout, 2–3 minutes on each side. Transfer peppers and fish to a cutting board and cut into strips.

Place 2 tortillas on each of 4 warmed individual plates. Divide peppers and fish evenly among tortillas. Top tacos with salsa and guacamole. Serve right away, garnished with cilantro and pass lime wedges for squeezing.

4 SERVINGS

Chicken Fajitas with Cabbage Slaw

chile powder
cumin
peppercorns

This recipe shows how, with a well-stocked spice pantry, you can make your own chili powder blend at home. Start with 2 parts of your favorite pure chile powder, add 1 part ground cumin and 1 part Mexican oregano. If you like it hot, add cayenne pepper to taste. Feel free to adjust the proportions as you like.

4 Tbsp (2 fl oz/60 ml) olive oil, plus more as needed

2 tsp ancho or New Mexico chile powder

1 tsp ground cumin

1 tsp dried oregano, crumbled

Cayenne pepper (optional)

1¼ lb (625 g) skinless, boneless chicken breasts

2 large red onions, halved and sliced lengthwise

Salt and freshly ground black peppercorns

8–12 small flour tortillas or corn tortillas

½ small head savoy cabbage, halved, cored, and thinly sliced

¼ cup (⅓ oz/10 g) chopped fresh cilantro

2 Tbsp fresh lime juice

1 large avocado, peeled, pitted, and sliced

In a large bowl, combine 2 tablespoons of oil, chile powder, cumin, oregano, and a pinch of cayenne, if using. Cut chicken crosswise into ½-inch (12-mm) slices. Add to bowl with seasonings. Add onions and toss to coat. Sprinkle with salt and black pepper. Set aside.

Preheat oven to 350°F (180°C). Wrap tortillas in foil and place in oven until heated through, about 15 minutes.

In another large bowl, combine cabbage and cilantro. Add remaining 2 tablespoons oil and toss to coat. Add lime juice and toss well. Season cabbage to taste with salt and black pepper. Transfer cabbage to a serving bowl. Arrange avocado slices in a small bowl.

Place 1 large griddle over 2 burners and warm over medium-high heat; brush with oil. Spread chicken and onions on griddle and cook, turning occasionally with tongs, until chicken is cooked through, about 5 minutes, and onions are brown, about 7 minutes.

Transfer chicken and onions to a warmed platter. Serve right away with warm tortillas, cabbage mixture, and avocados.

3 green onions, chopped

4 large cloves garlic, chopped

3 habanero chiles, seeded and chopped

¼ cup (2 fl oz/60 ml) fresh lime juice

3 Tbsp olive oil

2 Tbsp tamari or soy sauce

1 Tbsp brown sugar

1 Tbsp chopped fresh thyme

2 tsp ground allspice

1 tsp ground nutmeg

½ tsp ground cinnamon

Salt and freshly ground black peppercorns

6 whole chicken legs, about 12 oz (375 g) each

6 SERVINGS

Caribbean-Style Jerk Chicken

allspice
cinnamon
nutmeg
peppercorns

In a blender or food processor, combine green onions, garlic, chiles, lime juice, oil, tamari, brown sugar, thyme, allspice, nutmeg, cinnamon, and 2 teaspoons each salt and pepper and process until smooth. Place chicken legs on a platter and coat evenly on all sides with mixture. Cover and refrigerate for at least 8 hours or up to overnight.

At least 30 minutes before you are ready to begin grilling, remove chicken from refrigerator.

Prepare a grill for indirect grilling (1 hot zone and 1 cool zone) over medium heat. Brush and oil grill rack.

Place chicken legs on grill rack directly over the heat and sear, turning once, until nicely browned, about 2 minutes on each side. Move chicken legs to the cool side of the grill, cover, and cook until firm when touched and an instant-read thermometer inserted into thickest part of thigh away from bone registers 170°F (77°C), about 30 minutes.

Transfer chicken to a platter and let rest for 10 minutes. Serve right away.

Jerk seasoning is a unique blend of fiery chiles and spices common in Jamaican cooking. The unexpected blend of ingredients in "jerked" foods is influenced by visitors from countries around the globe, but the allspice is native to the island. Serve with fruit salsa, such as pineapple or mango.

Grilled Skirt Steak with Chimichurri

chile flakes
peppercorns
sweet paprika

1 cup (1 oz/30 g) fresh flat-leaf parsley leaves

½ cup (4 fl oz/125 ml) red wine vinegar

4 cloves garlic, minced

1 tsp dried oregano

1 tsp sweet paprika

¼ tsp chile flakes, or to taste

Salt and freshly ground black peppercorns

½ cup (4 fl oz/125 ml) olive oil, plus more for brushing

1 skirt steak, about 3 lb (1.5 kg)

In a food processor, combine parsley, vinegar, garlic, oregano, paprika, chile flakes, ½ teaspoon salt, and ¼ teaspoon pepper and process until parsley and garlic are uniformly minced, about 10 seconds. Transfer to a bowl and stir in ½ cup oil. Let stand at room temperature for at least 1 hour to allow flavors to blend. Bring steak to room temperature before grilling.

Prepare a grill for direct grilling over high heat. Brush and oil grill rack.

Brush steak with oil and season generously with salt. Place on grill rack directly over hot coals or heat elements and grill for 1–2 minutes on each side for medium-rare. Transfer steak to a carving board, tent with aluminum foil, and let rest for about 5 minutes.

Carve steak across grain into thin slices and serve right away with chimichurri sauce.

Chimichurri is as ubiquitous in Argentina as is tomato ketchup in North America—it is seen everywhere. While essentially a garlic and fresh herb salsa, Argentinian cooks customize their own versions with paprika or chile powder and spicy chile flakes, depending on their preference for heat.

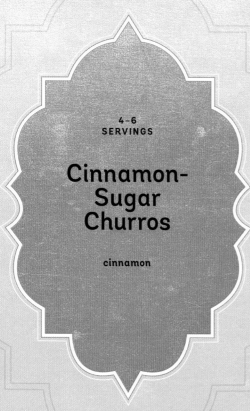

4–6 SERVINGS

Cinnamon-Sugar Churros

cinnamon

Churros are Mexican street food, often presented in a paper bag and served with a steaming cup of cinnamon-scented hot chocolate. While the use of the spice is prolific in Mexican cooking, so-called "Mexican cinnamon" in stores is more likely to be Ceylon cinnamon, which has been exported from Asia.

1 teaspoon salt
3 Tbsp sugar
1 cup (5 oz/155 g) all-purpose flour, sifted
2 large eggs, beaten
Canola oil for frying
1 Tbsp ground cinnamon

In a saucepan, combine 1 cup (8 fl oz/250 ml) water, salt, and 1 tablespoon of sugar. Bring to a boil over high heat, then remove from heat and immediately add flour all at once. Beat with a wooden spoon until dough is very smooth and pulls away from pan, about 2 minutes. Let cool for 5 minutes, then beat in eggs, about 1 tablespoon at a time. When eggs are thoroughly incorporated, spoon dough into a pastry bag fitted with a large star tip and twist bag closed.

Pour oil to a depth of 1 inch (2.5 cm) into a heavy frying pan and place over medium heat until a deep-frying thermometer reads about 350°F (180°C).

Pipe several strips of dough, each 3–4 inches (7.5–10 cm) long, directly into hot oil, being careful not to crowd pan. Cut dough strips from piping tip with a knife or scissors, dripping tool in oil before each cut. Fry churros, turning as needed, until deep golden brown and very crisp, 3–5 minutes. Using a slotted spoon or tongs, transfer to paper towels to drain briefly, then place in a large bowl. Repeat to cook remaining churros, letting the oil come back to 350°F before continuing.

In a small bowl, stir together cinnamon and remaining 2 tablespoons sugar. Add to bowl with warm churros and toss to coat evenly. Serve right away.

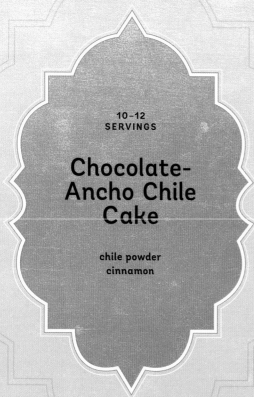

10–12 SERVINGS

Chocolate-Ancho Chile Cake

chile powder
cinnamon

Nonstick vegetable oil cooking spray

2 Tbsp ancho chile powder

1 tablet (3 oz/90 g) Mexican chocolate, coarsely chopped

1 cup (5½ oz/170 g) blanched almonds, toasted

⅓ cup (2 oz/60 g) all-purpose flour, sifted

¼ cup (¾ oz/20 g) Dutch-process cocoa powder, sifted

½ tsp ground cinnamon

½ cup (4 oz/125 g) unsalted butter, at room temperature

1 cup (8 oz/250 g) granulated sugar

6 large eggs, separated, at room temperature

1 Tbsp Kahlúa or crème de cacao

¼ tsp almond extract

Pinch of salt

1⅔ cup (13 fl oz/410 ml) heavy cream

1 Tbsp vanilla extract

3 Tbsp confectioners' sugar

Finely grated bittersweet chocolate for garnish

Preheat oven to 350°F (180°C). Line bottom of a round springform pan 9 inches (23 cm) in diameter and 2½ inches (6 cm) deep with parchment paper. Lightly coat sides of pan with cooking spray.

Reserve 1 teaspoon of chile powder for whipped cream. In a food processor, combine chocolate and almonds and pulse to grind finely. Transfer to a medium bowl; add flour, cocoa, remaining ground chile, and cinnamon and whisk to mix. In a large bowl, using an electric mixer on medium speed, beat butter until pale, about 2 minutes. Reduce speed to low and gradually add ½ cup (4 oz/125 g) of granulated sugar, stopping mixer at times to scrape down sides of bowl. Increase speed to medium and beat until mixture is light and fluffy, 3–5 minutes. Add egg yolks one at a time, beating until mixture is smooth, stopping to scrape down sides of bowl.

With mixer on low speed, add chocolate mixture, Kahlúa, and almond extract and beat just until blended.

In a large bowl, combine egg whites and salt. Using clean beaters, beat on medium speed for 30 seconds. Increase

This rich, chile-spiked chocolate cake is a Latin-style twist on a crowd-pleasing dessert. The addition of ancho chile powder lends a slightly fruity, earthy, and mildly spicy accent to the cake, which is garnished with chile-spiked whipped cream. The Mexican chocolate used in the cake also features a measure of cinnamon.

speed to high and beat until soft peaks form. With mixer running, add remaining ½ cup granulated sugar in a slow stream. Beat until stiff, shiny peaks form. Using a large rubber spatula, gently fold one-third of whites into batter. Fold in remaining whites in 2 batches just until combined.

Transfer batter to prepared pan and smooth surface. Place pan on a baking sheet to catch any drips. Bake cake until a toothpick comes out clean, 40–45 minutes. Transfer to a wire rack and let cool for 15 minutes, then release sides of pan and lift off. Let cake cool completely.

In a small bowl, whisk together ⅓ cup (3 fl oz/80 ml) of cream and reserved 1 teaspoon chile powder. Let stand for 5 minutes. Whisk again and pour into a chilled large bowl. Add remaining 1⅓ cups (10 fl oz/330 ml) cream and vanilla extract and, using an electric mixer on low speed, beat until cream thickens. Increase speed to medium-high and beat until soft peaks form. Reduce speed to medium and gradually add confectioners' sugar, beating until soft mounds form and cream is thick enough to hold its shape. Slice cake and place each slice on a plate. Add a dollop of whipped cream, top with grated chocolate, and serve right away.

Squat, brownish-red ancho chiles are the dried version of poblano chiles. Ground to a powder, they make a versatile spice to keep in the pantry to use for chili, spiced roasted vegetables, and, if you enjoy a little kick with your sweets, even desserts.

North America

Shrimp Boil with Corn
& Potatoes 95

Spice-Crusted Panfried Fish 96

Spicy Buttermilk Fried Chicken 97

Texas-Style Beef Chili 98

Spice-Rubbed Baby Back Ribs 101

Classic Dill Pickles 102

Sesame-Cheddar Wafers 104

Spiced Vegetable Slaw 105

Sugar-and-Spice Apple
Crumb Pie 107

Shrimp Boil with Corn & Potatoes

Atlantic seafood seasoning peppercorns

⅓ cup (3 fl oz/80 ml) cider vinegar

3 Tbsp Atlantic seafood seasoning blend such as Old Bay, plus more for sprinkling

Salt and freshly ground black peppercorns

1 lemon, quartered

2 lb (1 kg) red-skinned potatoes

1 lb (500 g) yellow onions, sliced

4 cloves garlic

6–8 ears corn, shucked and halved

4 lb (2 kg) head-on or 3 lb (1.5 kg) headless medium shrimp in the shell

Prepared tartar sauce or mayonnaise

Add 8 qt (8 l) water to a large nonreactive stockpot, making sure water does not fill pot more than two-thirds full. Add vinegar, seafood seasoning, 3 tablespoons salt, and lemon quarters. Cover pot and bring to a rolling boil over high heat.

When water is boiling, add potatoes, onions, and garlic to pot, cover, and return to a boil. Reduce heat to medium and cook until potatoes are nearly tender when pierced with tip of a paring knife, about 15 minutes. Add corn, re-cover, and cook for 5 minutes longer.

Remove pot from heat. Add shrimp, re-cover, and let stand until the shrimp are bright pink on outside and opaque throughout, about 5 minutes. Meanwhile, set a large colander in sink.

When shrimp are done, drain contents of pot thoroughly in colander. Pour shrimp and vegetables into a large tray or serving bowl and sprinkle with additional seafood seasoning and a few grinds of pepper. Serve right away, passing tartar sauce for dipping shrimp. Set a large bowl in center of table for shrimp shells and corncobs and set out plenty of napkins.

Cooks in the Mid-Atlantic states use a proprietary blend of spices and herbs, (commercially available as Old Bay seasoning) with abandon on all manner of shellfish native to the region. Like in other parts of the world, some households blend their own mixture to suit their familial tastes.

Spice-Crusted Panfried Fish

**black & white peppercorns
chile powder
garlic powder
sweet paprika**

½ tsp New Mexico chile powder

½ tsp sweet paprika

¼ tsp dried thyme

⅛ tsp garlic powder

Salt and freshly ground black peppercorns

¼ teaspoon freshly ground white peppercorns

4 striped bass or other firm white fish fillets, 6 oz (185 g) each, pin bones removed

2 Tbsp olive oil

Juice from 1 lemon

2 Tbsp unsalted butter, cut into pieces

In a small bowl, combine chile powder, paprika, thyme, garlic powder, ½ teaspoon salt, ¼ teaspoon black pepper, and white pepper. Place fillets on a plate and season on both sides with spice mixture.

In a large frying pan, heat olive oil over medium heat. Add fish and cook until well browned on first side, about 4 minutes. Turn and cook until opaque throughout, 2–4 minutes longer, depending on thickness. Transfer fillets to individual plates.

Wipe any oil from pan with a paper towel. Return pan to medium heat, add lemon juice and 1–2 tablespoons water and stir, scraping up any browned bits from pan bottom. Stir in butter until melted and season to taste with salt and pepper. Spoon sauce over fish and serve right away.

This recipe embraces the Cajun and Creole cooking traditions of the American South, which is influenced by African, French, and Spanish cooking. Based on chef Paul Prudhomme's famous blackened fish recipe from the 1980s, this is modernized with a lighter coating of spices and a quick lemon-butter sauce for a touch of easy elegance.

4 cups (32 fl oz/1 l) buttermilk

¼ cup (2½ oz/75 g) table salt

1 Tbsp hot red pepper sauce

1 chicken, about 4 lb (2 kg), cut into 10 pieces

1 cup (5 oz/155 g) all-purpose flour

¾ tsp baking powder

½ tsp freshly ground black peppercorns

¼ tsp cayenne pepper

½ tsp dried rosemary, crushed

½ tsp dried thyme

½ tsp dried sage

Canola oil for frying

4 SERVINGS

Spicy Buttermilk Fried Chicken

cayenne
peppercorns

In a very large nonreactive bowl, make a brine by whisking together buttermilk, salt, and red pepper sauce until salt dissolves. Add chicken, making sure that it is completely submerged. Cover and refrigerate for 6–12 hours. Remove bowl from refrigerator about 1 hour before you plan to fry.

Line a rimmed baking sheet with parchment paper. In a shallow dish, whisk together flour, baking powder, black pepper, cayenne, rosemary, thyme, and sage. One piece at a time, remove chicken from brine, shaking off excess, and roll in seasoned flour until completely coated. Place coated chicken on lined baking sheet.

In a large, deep frying pan, preferably cast iron, pour oil to a depth of 1 inch (2.5 cm) and heat over high heat until a deep-frying thermometer reads 350°F (180°C). Preheat oven to 350°F (180°C).

When oil is ready, using tongs, carefully add drumsticks and thighs to hot oil and fry until undersides are golden brown, about 4 minutes. Using tongs, turn and cook until second sides are golden brown, about 4 minutes longer. Transfer pieces to a rimmed baking sheet and bake for 10 minutes. Fry breast pieces and wings in same manner, then add to baking sheet with legs. Bake all pieces until opaque in center when pierced with a small knife, about 10 minutes longer.

Drain chicken briefly on paper towels and serve right away.

Southern cooks love deep-fried chicken. This version features a large measure of both black and cayenne peppers, and an array of dried herbs, to add lively flavors to the crisp coating that cloaks the chicken. Soaking the pieces in a buttermilk brine both adds flavor and keeps the chicken moist during frying.

8 SERVINGS

Texas-Style Beef Chili

chile powder
cumin
peppercorns
smoked paprika

In Texas, chili is made from beef, vegetables, and spices, period. Cooks there consider the addition of beans or tomatoes akin to sacrilege. This version uses hand-toasted and ground cumin seeds and fruity ancho chile powder, both authentic additions, then adds Spanish-style smoked paprika to the mix for a satisfying bowl of red.

2 tsp cumin seeds

¼ cup (1 oz/30 g) ancho chile powder

1 Tbsp Spanish smoked paprika

2 tsp dried oregano

4 lb (2 kg) boneless beef chuck roast, cubed

Salt and freshly ground black peppercorns

3 Tbsp olive oil

1 large yellow onion, chopped

1 fresh jalapeño chile, seeded and chopped

1 large red bell pepper, seeded and chopped

4 cloves garlic, minced

1½ cups (12 fl oz/375 ml) lager beer

1 cup (8 fl oz/250 ml) beef broth

2 Tbsp yellow cornmeal

Slivered red onions and chopped pickled jalapeño chiles for serving

In a small frying pan, toast cumin seeds over medium heat, shaking pan occasionally, until fragrant, about 2 minutes. Transfer to a mortar and finely grind with a pestle (or use a spice grinder). Transfer to a bowl and add chile powder, paprika, and oregano. Mix well and set aside.

Season beef with salt and pepper. In a Dutch oven, heat 2 tablespoons of oil over medium-high heat. In batches to avoid crowding, add beef cubes and cook, turning occasionally, until browned, about 5 minutes per batch. Transfer to a plate.

Add remaining 1 tablespoon oil to pot. Add onion, fresh chile, bell pepper, and garlic and reduce heat to medium. Cover and cook, stirring occasionally, until onion softens, about 5 minutes. Uncover, add spice mixture, and stir well for 30 seconds. Stir in beer and broth. Return beef to pot, cover, and reduce heat to low. Simmer until beef is fork-tender, 1½–2 hours.

Remove chili from heat and let stand for 5 minutes. Skim off any fat that rises to surface. Return pot to medium heat and bring to a simmer. Transfer about ½ cup (4 fl oz/125 ml) of cooking liquid to a small bowl, add cornmeal, and whisk well. Stir into chili and cook until lightly thickened, about 1 minute. Season to taste with salt and pepper. Spoon chili into warmed bowls and serve right away topped with onions and pickled jalapeños.

Spice-Rubbed Baby Back Ribs

chile powder
cumin
garlic powder
paprika
peppercorns

½ cup (4 oz/125 g) sweet or hot paprika

2 Tbsp brown sugar

1 Tbsp ancho or New Mexico chile powder

1 Tbsp garlic powder

1 tsp dry mustard

1 tsp ground cumin

Kosher salt and freshly ground black peppercorns

4 slabs baby back pork ribs, about 5 lb (2.5 kg), trimmed

Prepared barbecue sauce

In a small bowl, stir together paprika, brown sugar, chile powder, garlic powder, mustard, cumin, 1 tablespoon salt, and 1 teaspoon pepper.

Rinse ribs under cold running water and pat dry with paper towels. Generously season all over with spice mixture, massaging it in well. Cover and refrigerate overnight.

Preheat oven to 350°F (180°C). Place ribs in a shallow roasting pan and roast, turning occasionally, until they are fork-tender, 2–2½ hours.

Prepare a grill for direct grilling over medium heat. Brush and oil grill rack.

Transfer ribs to a cutting board and cut each slab into 3- or 4-rib portions. Brush with barbecue sauce on both sides. Place ribs on grill rack directly over hot coals or heat elements and cook, turning once, until shiny and glazed, about 5 minutes per side. If barbecue sauce begins to burn, transfer ribs to a cooler area of grill.

Transfer ribs to a cutting board. Cut ribs between bones and pile high on a platter. Serve right away with additional barbecue sauce on side.

This is a hybrid recipe for ribs, fusing the dry-rub method of Memphis-style barbecue with the sauce-slathered style of Kansas City fare. The ribs are first coated with a spice rub and refrigerated overnight, then partially cooked in the oven until tender. Just before serving, they are coated with sauce and finished on the grill.

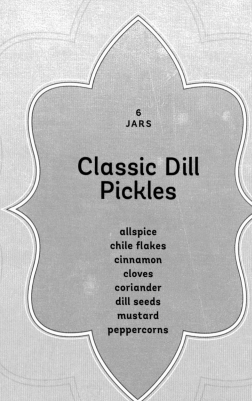

6 JARS

Classic Dill Pickles

allspice
chile flakes
cinnamon
cloves
coriander
dill seeds
mustard
peppercorns

3 cups (24 fl oz/750 ml) distilled white vinegar
2 Tbsp salt
6 Tbsp pickling spice (see Note)
6 Tbsp dill seeds
24 fresh dill sprigs

24 cloves garlic
36 black peppercorns
6 lb (3 kg) Kirby cucumbers, each about 1½ inches (4 cm) in diameter, halved lengthwise

Have ready 6 hot, sterilized 1 pint (500 ml) canning jars and their lids. Fill a canning pot two-thirds full with water and bring to a boil over high heat. Meanwhile, in a large nonreactive saucepan, combine vinegar and salt. Add 3 cups (24 fl oz/750 ml) water and bring to a boil over medium-high heat, stirring to dissolve salt.

In each jar, place 1 tablespoon pickling spice, 1 tablespoon dill seeds, 4 dill sprigs, 4 garlic cloves, and 6 peppercorns. Place cucumber halves in sterilized jars, making sure to pack them tightly and avoid large gaps. Fill jars to within ¾ inch (2 cm) of rims. Ladle hot vinegar brine into jars, leaving ½ inch (12 mm) of space at top. Run a thin nonmetallic spatula or a chopstick around inside edge of each jar to release any air bubbles trapped inside, and add more brine if necessary to reach within ¾ inch (2 cm) of rim. Wipe rims clean and seal tightly with lids.

Immediately arrange jars in canning pot. Do not let jars cool before exposing them to boiling water or they may crack. Make sure jars are covered by at least 2 inches (5 cm) of water. Cover pot with lid and process jars for 7 minutes, beginning timing after water has returned to a rapid boil. Remove jars from boiling water and place them on a kitchen towel or rack.

When jars have cooled completely, gently press on top of each lid. It should be taut and slightly indented. If lid bounces back and makes a clicking noise when you press it, the seal is not good. Let jars stand undisturbed for 24 hours and then set aside for 2 weeks for flavors to develop. Sealed jars can be stored in a cool, dark place for up to 1 year. If a seal has failed, store jar in refrigerator for up to 1 week.

Pickling spice is available in stores, but with a well-stocked spice cabinet, it's easy to make your own: Mix 1 cinnamon stick, broken into pieces; 2 bay leaves, crushed; 2 cloves; 2 tablespoons *each* mustard and coriander seeds; 1 tablespoon mixed peppercorns, 2 teaspoons *each* whole allspice and dill seeds; and 1 teaspoon red chile flakes.

Sesame-Cheddar Wafers

cayenne
cumin
sesame seeds

1½ cups (7½ oz/235 g)
all-purpose flour

1 cup (4 oz/125 g) grated
Parmesan cheese

1 cup (4 oz/125 g) shredded
sharp Cheddar cheese

⅓ cup (1 oz/30 g)
sesame seeds

1 tsp ground cumin

½ tsp salt

¼ tsp cayenne pepper

½ cup (4 oz/125 g) plus
2 Tbsp chilled unsalted
butter, cut into pieces

This recipe comes from the American South, where sesame seeds play a role in the regional cuisine. Sesame seeds were first brought to the New World on slave ships, and many Southerners still call them by their African name, *benne.* These easy, savory crackers are great to serve with drinks at a cocktail party.

In a food processor, combine flour, Parmesan cheese, Cheddar cheese, sesame seeds, cumin, salt, cayenne pepper, and butter. Process until mixture is well combined but crumbly and holds together when squeezed with your hand, about 2 minutes.

Transfer mixture to a lightly floured work surface and knead gently until dough comes together and holds its shape. Then, using your hands, roll dough into a log about 12 inches (30 cm) long and about 1½ inches (4 cm) in diameter. Wrap in plastic wrap and refrigerate until firm, at least 3 hours or up to 24 hours.

Preheat the oven to 375°F (190°C). Line 2 baking sheets with parchment paper.

Remove dough log from refrigerator and, working quickly, use a sharp knife to cut into slices ¼ inch (6 mm) thick. Arrange slices about 1 inch (2.5 cm) apart on prepared baking sheets.

Bake until edges appear crisp and brown, about 10 minutes. Let cool on sheets for about 12 minutes, then transfer wafers to wire racks to cool completely. Wafers can be stored in an airtight container for up to 1 week.

Spiced Vegetable Slaw

Atlantic seafood seasoning peppercorns

1 head green cabbage, about 2 lb (1 kg)

2 large carrots, peeled

2 Tbsp white wine vinegar

1 large red bell pepper

4 green onions, finely chopped

1 cup (8 fl oz/250 ml) good-quality mayonnaise

1 Tbsp Atlantic seafood seasoning blend, such as Old Bay

Salt and freshly ground black peppercorns

Cut cabbage into wedges. Cut out and discard core. Using a large knife, cut the cabbage crosswise into fine shreds. Transfer to a large bowl.

Using the large holes on a grater-shredder, shred carrots and add to bowl with cabbage. Sprinkle cabbage and carrots with vinegar and mix well.

Seed bell pepper and cut into thin strips. Stir bell pepper and green onions into bowl with cabbage and carrots.

Add mayonnaise and seafood seasoning and mix well. Taste and adjust the seasoning with salt and pepper. Cover and refrigerate until chilled, at least 2 hours. Serve cold.

Coleslaw is a popular side dish for fish and shellfish, so it makes sense to season it with the ubiquitous seafood seasoning blend from the coastal Atlantic states. The mayonnaise helps carry the flavors of the spices. You can also use the seasoning to flavor mayonnaise for dipping sauces or sandwich spreads.

Pie dough for a 9-inch (23-cm) pie, rolled out

½ cup (2½ oz/75 g) all-purpose flour

⅓ cup (2½ oz/75 g) firmly packed brown sugar

3 tsp ground cinnamon

Salt

5 Tbsp (2½ oz/75 g) cold unsalted butter, cut into pieces

7 large, tart, firm apples, peeled and sliced

1 tablespoon fresh lemon juice

⅓ cup (3 oz/90 g) granulated sugar

2 tablespoons cornstarch

½ teaspoon freshly grated nutmeg

¼ teaspoon ground allspice

Pinch of ground cloves

8 SERVINGS

Sugar-and-Spice Apple Crumb Pie

**allspice
cinnamon
cloves
nutmeg**

Fold dough round in half and carefully transfer to a 9-inch (23-cm) pie dish. Unfold and ease dough into dish. Using kitchen scissors, trim edge, leaving ¾ inch (2 cm) of overhang. Fold overhang under itself and pinch it together to create a high edge on the dish's rim. Flute edge decoratively.

To make topping, in a small bowl, stir together flour, brown sugar, 2 teaspoons of cinnamon, and ¼ teaspoon salt. Using a pastry blender, cut in butter until the mixture is crumbly. Cover and chill in the refrigerator until ready to use.

To make filling, place apples in a large bowl, sprinkle with lemon juice, and toss to coat evenly. In small bowl, stir together granulated sugar, cornstarch, remaining 1 teaspoon cinnamon, nutmeg, allspice, cloves, and a pinch of salt. Sprinkle sugar mixture over apples and toss to distribute evenly. Transfer to dough-lined pan and sprinkle evenly with crumb topping.

Refrigerate pie until the dough is firm, 20–30 minutes. Meanwhile, preheat oven to 375°F (190°C).

Bake pie until crust is golden and filling is bubbling underneath topping, 50–60 minutes. Transfer to rack and let cool completely. Serve at room temperature or rewarm in a 350°F (180°C) oven for 10–15 minutes. Cut into wedges to serve.

It's possible to buy pre-mixed spice blends called "Apple Pie Spice" or "Pumpkin Pie Spice" for your holiday pies, but doing so means you have no idea how old the spices are and what are the proportions of spices inside. This pie features a quartet of traditional fall spices, the amounts of which you can customize to your own taste.

INDEX

weldon**owen**

415 Jackson Street, Suite 200, San Francisco, CA 94111
Telephone: 415 291 0100 Fax: 415 291 8841
www.weldonowen.com

Weldon Owen is a division of
BONNIER

WELDON OWEN, INC.

CEO and President Terry Newell
VP, Sales and Marketing Amy Kaneko
Director of Finance Mark Perrigo

VP and Publisher Hannah Rahill

Creative Director Emma Boys
Senior Art Director Kara Church
Art Director Alexandra Zeigler

Production Director Chris Hemesath
Production Manager Michelle Duggan

Photographer Maren Caruso
Food Stylist Robyn Valarik
Prop Stylist Mindi Shapiro

COOKING WITH SPICE

Conceived and produced by Weldon Owen, Inc.
Copyright © 2012 Weldon Owen, Inc.

All rights reserved, including the right of
reproduction in whole or in part in any form.

Printed and bound by 1010 Printing, Ltd. in China

First printed in 2012
10 9 8 7 6 5 4 3 2 1

Library of Congress Cataloging-in-Publication
data is available

ISBN-13: 978-1-61628-483-1
ISBN-10: 1-61628-483-8

ACKNOWLEDGMENTS

Weldon Owen wishes to thank the following people for their generous support
in producing this book: Lauren Charles, Sean Franzen, Anna Grace, Erin Kunkel,
Rachel Lopez Metzger, Elizabeth Parson, Jane Tunks, Jason Wheeler, Sharron Wood

PHOTO CREDITS

All photographs by Maren Caruso except pages 18, 51, and 68 by Erin Kunkel